W9-BRM-852

CATFANCY

Naughty
no
more!

Change Unwanted Behaviors
through Positive Reinforcement

by
Marilyn Krieger

Lead Editor: Jennifer Calvert
Editor: Amy Deputato
Art Director: Jerome Callens
Production Supervisor: Jessica Jaensch
Assistant Production Manager: Tracy Vogtman
Indexer: Melody Englund

Vice President, Chief Content Officer: June Kikuchi
Vice President, Kennel Club Books: Andrew DePrisco
BowTie Press: Jennifer Calvert, Amy Deputato,
Karen Julian, Jarelle S. Stein

Text Copyright © 2010 by BowTie Press®

All rights reserved. No part of this book may be reproduced, stored in
a retrieval system, or transmitted in any form or by any means, electronic, mechanical, photocopying, recording, or otherwise, without the
prior written permission of BowTie Press®, except for the inclusion of
brief quotations in an acknowledged review.

Library of Congress Cataloging-in-Publication Data

Krieger, Marilyn, 1953-
  CAT FANCY's Naughty No More! / by Marilyn Krieger.
      p. cm.
  Includes bibliographical references.
  ISBN 978-1-933958-92-7
  1. Cats--Training. 2. Clicker training (Animal training) I.
Title.
  SF446.6.K75 2010
  636.8'0835--dc22

                            2010002549

BowTie Press®
A Division of BowTie, Inc.
3 Burroughs
Irvine, California 92618

Printed and bound in United States
16 15 14 13 12   3 4 5 6 7 8 9 10

Dedication

To my late father,
Charles H. Krieger (1923–2009),
a wonderful man who will live forever
in our memories.

He always said that I could do
anything I set my mind to.

Acknowledgments

There are many special people who, through their support and encouragement, played a major role in the process of building this book. Foremost among them are my parents, Charles and June Krieger; my sister, Carol Krieger; and my brother-in-law, Geoffrey Neate. Their comments and suggestions were very valuable and very much appreciated. Sadly, my father passed on before the completion of CAT FANCY's *Naughty No More!*.

A special thanks goes to my dear friend and mentor, Pam Johnson-Bennett, who reviewed my chapters and encouraged me every step of the way. She's been with me from the beginning of my journey, and patiently listened to me obsess about details. I treasure her friendship and guidance and immensely enjoy our discussions about behavior. Thanks also to Frances Byrne for her valuable guidance, marketing expertise, encouragement, and friendship. I thank Bob Bailey, Alexandra Kurland, and Dr. Susan Friedman, as well, for graciously sharing their remarkable knowledge about animal behavior and training with me.

All cats deserve recognition; they are perfect and good. Everything about them, from their elegance to their fascinating behaviors and the mysteries associated with them throughout history, inspired me to pursue a career in cat behavior and write CAT FANCY's *Naughty No More!*. The cats who particularly deserve kudos are the special little ones I share my life with. Maulee, Sudan, Jinniyha, Olivia, Kingsley, and Asia are the true stars of CAT FANCY's *Naughty No More!,* and they deserve extra-delicious treats and lots of attention for their roles in the creation of this book. They are especially perfect cats.

Contents

Foreword

When I started doing behavior consultations over twenty years ago, it was so difficult to convince people that cats could be trained. Dogs were the trainable animals, I was repeatedly told, but cats were stubborn creatures with minds of their own. As a result of that thinking, many cats ended up being abandoned, relinquished to shelters, or euthanized for behavior problems. It's very sad to think of the unfair treatment cats have endured when in fact they are extremely trainable. These beautiful, intelligent creatures are easy to communicate with and are highly motivated. It just takes the right tools.

Operant conditioning (clicker training) is the key to solving current behavior problems, preventing future behavior issues, and improving the relationship you share with your cat. By using clicker training, you and your cat change your mindsets from negative to positive. Through this method, you're able to actually provide a roadmap for your cat toward good behavior while meeting her needs at the same time.

Regardless of how frustrating your cat's behavior problem is, it serves a purpose. Animals don't repeat behaviors if they don't serve a function. By using operant conditioning and following the steps mapped out in CAT FANCY's *Naughty No More!,* you can figure out what need a particular behavior is filling (in other words, the "pay off"), provide a more acceptable alternative for your cat, and then reward him when he chooses the better option. The additional benefit of this technique is that it's actually fun for both you and your cat. Instead of having the relationship become strained and tense due to counter-productive training or punishment, you'll find yourself enjoying your cat again. What's more, your cat will start enjoying *you* again. You'll get back to the way you wanted the relationship to be in the first place. Clicker training is a serious, science-based behavior modification method disguised as fun. It's a win/win situation for the cat and her human family.

Clicker training isn't a new concept, but it has been a training method used more popularly with dogs. Those of us who work with cats know how effective clicker training is with felines, but many cat owners are still unaware of the technique. Once you learn about it, you'll feel as if you've found the key that unlocks many doors. It's that powerful!

Because clicker training for cats isn't as well known as it is for dogs, there has been very little authoritative information out there for cat owners...until now. CAT FANCY's *Naughty No More!* provides you with an excellent foundation for improving your cat's behavior. Marilyn Krieger leads you on a fun ride through cat behavior with the help of her trusty clicker.

Pam Johnson-Bennett
Certified Animal Behavior
Consultant
Author of seven titles,
including
Starting from Scratch,
Cat vs. Cat, and
Think Like a Cat

Introduction

I wrote this book from the trenches. I've had personal hands-on experience with every one of the challenges described in CAT FANCY's *Naughty No More!*—my cats all had their special behavior problems. They have helped me test and develop solutions that work. The behavior challenges that I haven't lived with, my clients have. All of the clicker solutions, along with the accompanying behavior recommendations, covered in this book have been successfully implemented on my clients' and my own cats.

My cats were, of course, my main inspiration for writing CAT FANCY's *Naughty No More!*. Living with the smartest and most mischievous cats in existence is very inspiring. (You will meet my little Einsteins and read about some of their antics throughout the pages of this book.) But the popular misconception that cats can't be trained convinced me further that I needed to write this book.

Historically, popular culture has dictated that cats will only do things on their own terms. Another widely held belief is that once a cat is repeatedly displaying undesirable behavior, the behavior can't be stopped. I recently watched a popular morning news show that compared cats and dogs. The hosts concluded that cats don't listen, that they do only what they want to do, and that it's impossible to train them. Unfortunately, these mistaken assumptions often result in cats being unnecessarily surrendered to shelters and euthanized because of resolvable behaviors such as inappropriate elimination, aggression, and furniture-scratching. These behaviors certainly aren't fun to live with, but they can be stopped using a combination of clicker training, behavior modification, and simple changes to the environment.

Clicker training is an effective training system, based on the science of operant conditioning, that rewards animals for appropriate activities and behaviors. This process uses the scientifically proven principle that animals (in our case, cats) are more apt to intentionally repeat an activity when it is immediately followed by a reward or other positive consequence. The cat understands that a behavior is the right one because a device—in this case, a clicker—is used to communicate that the behavior is correct as it is being performed.

The first step of clicker training is establishing an association between the sound of the clicker and something the cat loves, such as a food treat. After the association has been made, the cat will know that whatever she is doing at the instant she hears the clicker is good. You'll find out more about the history and science of both operant conditioning and clicker training in the first chapter and in the time line at the back of CAT FANCY's *Naughty No More!*.

Clicker training, combined with other positive techniques, is effective for a number of reasons. It replaces unwanted behaviors with more acceptable activities that are also more fun for the cat. Additionally, clicker training can increase a cat's sense of security and can build trust and affection between cats and their people. An added benefit is that this kind of training is mentally stimulating and challenging for the cat. And all of this can be done without punishment.

I cringe when I hear about any animal being punished. Too many people use punishment such as hitting, yelling, forcefulness, and fear tactics in attempts to change their cats' behavior. However, punishment is likely to escalate the unwanted activity, create other problem behaviors, or result in the cat avoiding her people. The positive methods detailed in CAT FANCY's *Naughty No More!* are more effective than punishment, are long-term, and are fun for everyone!

So why do cats sometimes exhibit unwanted behaviors? Do they wake up one day after a nap and randomly decide to engage in what we see as inappropriate activity? And what can we do to change those behaviors? In 2009, I had the good fortune of attending a talk given by Dr. Susan Friedman, a highly respected behavior analyst who teaches behavior basics to animal behaviorists. She pointed out that animals don't behave randomly. Dr. Friedman says, "It's always about environmental management. Our job as caregivers is to arrange the environment so that the right behavior is easier than the wrong behavior and is more rewarding." Cats, like all animals, always have reasons for their behavior. What people perceive as bad behavior is often a response to stimuli or something in the environment. But the good news is that you can manage the cat's environment and can change or eliminate the unappreciated activities without the use of punishment.

Knowing that the cat has a reason to urinate on the couch doesn't make the act acceptable and certainly won't make the problem go away. That's where this book helps—by giving you insights into why your cat is engaged in the unpleasant behavior and then providing you with solutions for changing or eliminating the behavior. A bonus is that you can teach your cat tricks. Although the focus of CAT FANCY's *Naughty No More!* is not on teaching tricks, chapter 10 gives step-by-step instructions for a number of impressive ones.

The next time you hear someone make a statement about the inability to train cats or change their behaviors, educate that person. Perhaps your actions will help save some cats from being surrendered to shelters or euthanized for unacceptable behaviors that can be corrected through clicker training, education, management, and behavior modification.

Cats Just Wanna Have Fun

Clicker training isn't the only training technique out there, but it is the best method for training cats. Reward-based methods have been scientifically proven to be more effective than fear-based methods in creating lasting behavioral changes. Clicker training is also fun, which means that the cat is usually eager to participate. This training method is also perfect for cats because they have a natural tendency to be a bit fearful in unfamiliar situations, and the process of clicker training encourages involvement and the exploration of new behaviors.

Clicker training is great for changing unwanted behaviors because it provides alternative activities for the cat, thereby focusing the cat on something other than the initial (undesirable) behavior.

BEGINNER'S TOOL KIT
- **Primary reinforcer** (delicious treats or regular food, or possibly affection or play)
- **Secondary reinforcer** (a device that makes a consistent sound: i-Click clicker, ballpoint pen for shy cats, or flashlight for a hearing-impaired cat)
- **Target prop** (a chopstick or a new pencil with an eraser on the end)
- **Placemat** or other moveable object for the cat to stand on

Additionally, it helps increase a cat's feelings of security, builds and strengthens bonds between cats and their people, and is a powerful communication tool.

Every journey begins with a single step, so the journey to clicking away unwanted behaviors starts with a single click. And while working toward better behavior, you can teach your cat impressive tricks that will astound the in-laws and amaze the neighbors. No one has to know that your cat now shakes hands because she used to be a door darter, ruined your couch, or disliked visitors.

But before your cat can start wowing crowds, you both need to learn the basics. The good news is that they are easy and fun to learn. Are you ready? Your clicker-training journey is about to begin.

Rule Number One: Make it Fun!

Clicker training should be fun for you and especially for your cat. If training becomes a chore, you won't want to spend your valuable time doing it—and neither will your cat. The beauty of clicker training is that it empowers the cat and allows her to progress at her own pace. When she's motivated and enjoying the challenge, she'll want more. When your cat gets bored with clicker-training sessions, you'll know it—she'll walk away, fixate on the fly on the wall, flop down, or display other behavior that communicates "I'm through." Respect her wishes and conduct another session later in the day or the next day.

Finding something that motivates your cat will help make clicker training fun for both of you. Cats, like people, are more likely to work at an activity that has a satisfying reward of some kind. I'll bet that if you had a boring job with inadequate pay, you would start updating your resume and checking the employment ads.

Some cats are motivated by play.

Motivate Me!

Most cats are motivated by food. For these cats (later referred to as "Foodies"), a small piece of a favorite treat acts as a perfect primary reinforcer. Treats should be tiny, about the size of half of a piece of dry food. Some cats only like their regular food and won't come within 10 feet of a treat, no matter how yummy you think it might be. For those cats who enjoy munching only on dry food, a treat can be half of a piece of their regular mealtime dry food. One lick from a spoon filled with their favorite canned food will work for cats who have a love affair with their canned food.

A word of advice: don't leave food out for your cat 24/7. Instead, feed a few meals during the day, picking the food up between the feedings. In addition, have a fixed feeding schedule; feed your cat at the same times every day. Cats who have access to their food all the time are more difficult to motivate. After all, why should they work for a treat when all they have to do is saunter over to their food bowl and have a snack?

Food isn't the only motivator, however. There are cats who aren't motivated by food at all. These eccentric cats might be motivated by affection or grooming. Cats who are motivated by affection respond to something like a cuddle, a stroke, or a kiss. Cats who love to be groomed can be rewarded with a couple of loving brushstrokes. It may take some experimentation and a little time to determine the best motivator for your cat. The right motivator is very important for making clicker training successful and fun for everyone.

Some cats are motivated by a food, others by affection or grooming.

A SPECIAL PLACE

Cats are easily sidetracked. It is important to train in a location without distractions such as other animals or loud noises, where your cat feels safe. The treats you are using as primary reinforcers should be the only food available during the training sessions.

B.F. SKINNER AND THE SCIENCE OF OPERANT CONDITIONING

B.F. Skinner in his lab

Clicker training is based on operant conditioning, a method of learning discovered through B.F. Skinner's meticulous research in the 1930s. Operant conditioning describes animals forming an association between a behavior they're doing and the consequences of that behavior. The consequences modify the behavior. In order to collect the data for his research, Skinner invented an apparatus called an operant conditioning chamber. The operant conditioning chamber was a box containing a lever and a food-delivery system. When a rat placed in the chamber without any stimuli accidentally bumped the lever, the action was reinforced and strengthened with a food pellet that was delivered mechanically. Realizing the delivery of the food pellet occurred immediately after he touched the lever, the rat began to bump the lever with increasing frequency. The rat's action changed from a random event to an intentional behavior.

During WWII, Skinner also worked with pigeons. The simple actions and responses of the rats and pigeons were recorded and measured by another invention of Skinner's—the cumulative recorder. The recorder documented the timing and frequency of the lever being pressed. The data that was collected showed that animals repeat behavior when there are positive consequences, or reinforcers, for the behavior. The data also showed that animals will stop behavior when it isn't reinforced.

The reinforcers that Skinner referred to throughout his experiments were activities or items that strengthened an animal's behavior. These were called primary and secondary reinforcers or conditioned reinforcers. Skinner typically used food as the primary reinforcer. An example of a secondary or conditioned reinforcer is the sound the food dispenser made just before the food—the primary reinforcer—was delivered. The animal associated that sound with the subsequent delivery of food.

Another aspect of operant conditioning is that animals won't repeat behaviors if there aren't any positive consequences or if there are negative consequences (punishment). However, Skinner's research showed how behavior can be easily and effectively changed without punishment.

The Essential Click, Bong, or Clink

Once you have a motivator, you need to find a device that will always perform the same action when it's activated. The action might be a sound, a vibration, or a flash of light. In clicker-training-speak, this device is called a *secondary reinforcer* or an *event marker* after it is paired with the primary motivator. This secondary reinforcer will then be used to communicate to your cat when she is doing something right. The most popular device that is used today for clicker training is the clicker. This is a small object with either a piece of metal or a button in the middle of it. When the metal piece or button is depressed it makes a clicking noise. I find that the most effective clicker is Karen Pryor's i-Click clicker. This clicker has a nice, soft sound and an excellent response time. When the button is depressed, the click is instantaneous; there is no lag between the act of clicking and the click. And with clicker training, timing is crucial!

When working with feral or shy kitties, the quieter sound of a ballpoint pen works well as the secondary reinforcer. Or you can try wrapping the clicker in a sock to produce a softer click. Hearing-impaired cats can also be clicker-trained. Instead of using a device that makes a noise, shine a quick flash of light from a pen light or a flashlight on the floor in front of the hearing-challenged kitty. Other creative marking devices are bells, rattles, or whistles. You really can use anything that makes

The i-Click clicker has a soft sound when it is activated.

MORE CLICKER-SPEAK: THREE TERMS FOR THE SAME DEVICE

Because a secondary reinforcer is used to tell your cat when she is doing something correct in the moment, it is sometimes called an *event marker*. The event marker "captures an event." When the clicker is activated, the click needs to occur at the exact instant of the behavior you are reinforcing. If you are late in clicking, then whatever your cat is doing at the moment of the click is what will be reinforced.

A secondary reinforcer is also sometimes called a *bridging stimulus* or *bridge* because it functions as a communication tool. It tells the cat that she is performing a behavior correctly and that she will be rewarded later with a treat for her correct behavior. The term *bridging stimulus* was coined by Keller Breland, one of the pioneers of clicker training.

THE POWER OF THE PEN

Retractable ballpoint pens can be good clickers for cats who are easily startled by noises. The only drawback to using a retractable ballpoint pen is that you have to make a conscious effort to not click the pen at other times, such as when you are using the pen for what it was originally intended. Make every click count!

an immediate and consistent sound. Toy stores have many types of toys that make all sorts of unique sounds. It's important to note that making vocal noises or tongue clicks is not recommended because those organic sounds are never the same each time.

Whatever device you do decide on, use it only when marking or reinforcing a behavior. It can become confusing for a cat if the clicker or pen is clicked or the bell is rung at random times, so make sure that the device is something that you don't normally use around the house. Its function will be fully dedicated to the clicker-training cause.

Conditioning the Secondary Reinforcer

The first task in clicker training is pairing the motivator with the device. In clicker-speak, this is called *conditioning the secondary reinforcer* or *charging the clicker.* The goal is for the cat to have a positive feeling whenever the secondary reinforcer is activated. Because clickers are commonly used, we will refer to the secondary reinforcer as a clicker, and because the majority of cats are Foodies, we will refer to the motivator as a treat.

Pairing the sound of the clicker with something positive—the food—is the first step toward changing unwanted behaviors. The clicker becomes a way to communicate to your cat when she is doing something you are happy with.

The process of charging the clicker, as Karen Pryor called it, is very easy. After clicking the device once, immediately toss the cat a small treat. Be sure to toss the treat to the cat as soon as possible after clicking. Wait until the cat has completely eaten the treat and looks back up at you before clicking again. It's important that the cat give you her undivided attention before you click

Pair the sound of the clicker with the treat by clicking and then immediately tossing or placing the treat in front of the cat.

again. Some cats enjoy vacuuming every crumb off the floor before they're ready for the next repetition. Many cats make the connection between the click and the treat within just a few repetitions; others take longer, sometimes needing twelve to twenty click-and-treat repetitions before they understand the association.

Don't forget rule number one! Clicker training is supposed to be fun for everyone. If your cat would rather gaze out the window and not work, then let her. Schedule another session a little later in the day. In the beginning, have multiple short sessions throughout the day. As both you and your cat become proficient in clicker language, the sessions should become longer. But it's completely up to the cat.

HISTORY OF THE CLICKER

By 1935, Skinner understood the practical applications of operant conditioning and the use of the secondary reinforcer for training animals. The secondary reinforcer Skinner first recognized and later introduced to Marian and Keller Breland, was the sound of the food dispenser in the operant conditioning chamber before it dispensed food. The Brelands and Skinner had different motivations. Skinner was interested primarily in research while the Brelands needed to find ways to train animals quickly and efficiently, based on the operant principles, in order to succeed as a business.

The Brelands realized that the secondary reinforcer (any device that performs the same action each time they're activated) could be used for building precision in behaviors and for effectively building and reinforcing behavior from a distance. The secondary reinforcer accurately marked a desired behavior at the precise moment it occurred, alerting the animal in the moment that he was doing a good job. It also signaled to the animal when a behavior was completed. Whistles and bells are two examples of secondary reinforcers used when working with marine mammals. Visual signal devices, such as penlights can be used to train hearing-impaired animals.

In late 1943, the Brelands started using party clickers for training animals. These were readily available before World War II but during the war were hard to find because metal was scarce. Meeting this challenge, the Brelands made clickers out of sticks with pieces of metal. Unfortunately, these experimental clickers were clumsy, so the Brelands searched for other secondary reinforcers and found horns and whistles worked well, especially over a distance.

In recent years, Karen Pryor designed the i-Click clicker, a clicker with a softer sound that immediately responds when activated.

CATS CAN'T FAIL

If your cat doesn't seem to "get it," consider the motivator. It is possible that your cat might not like whatever you are trying to motivate her with. If that's not the problem, consider your cat's routine. Don't try clicker training a cat right after she's eaten. If she's just had a satisfying meal, she won't be particularly motivated by treats. Besides, after eating, the first item on her agenda will probably be to take a nap. A better time to clicker train is before a meal, when your cat is hungry, easily motivated, and ready to work.

First Behavior: Please Touch the Target

One of the secrets to clicker training is to keep it simple and build from what's been learned. After pairing the clicker with something motivating, request a simple behavior that both you and your cat can learn from. The goal of this first behavior is for the cat to simply touch her nose to a specified object or prop, otherwise known in clicker-speak as a *target*. The target can be a chopstick or the eraser end of a new pencil. Pencils make wonderful targets because the eraser on the end resembles a cat's nose; when friendly cats greet each other, they usually touch each other's noses. A long stick with a ball stuck on the end can be a good target for shy or scared cats.

Start by holding the target in one hand. In the other hand, hold the clicker and the treats. Don't hold the target and the clicker in the same hand because the vibration from the click occurring next to the target can startle the cat. It is important that you have a large supply of treats nearby in a closed container. The

Hold the target in one hand and the clicker and treats in the other.

treats should always be within easy reach in order to maintain a rhythm when training. A dog-treat pouch that is worn around the waist is perfect for the job. For a cat motivated by grooming or play, you should have her toys or grooming tools placed within your reach.

Lower the target to your cat's nose level, about $\frac{1}{2}$ to 1 inch away from her nose so that she'll have to stretch a little to touch it. Her automatic response should be to touch it with her nose. As she touches it, click once and then immediately toss her the treat. Timing is essential. Click simultaneously as she touches the target. Don't click a quarter of a second after or before she touches it. The click is functioning as an event marker, communicating to your cat that the action she is doing at the time of the click is good and will be rewarded. Toss her the treat only after the touch/click. The click strengthens the target-touching behavior because the sound of the clicker has been paired with something wonderful—a treat.

You are ready to repeat the cycle only after your cat finishes her treat and looks back up at you. Separate each target/click/treat cycle by raising the target up above your cat's line of sight between cycles. You may find that your cat occasionally doesn't touch the target. If that's the case, don't click and treat when she doesn't touch it; simply reset by lifting the target up, out of her range of vision, and then lowering it again for her to touch. It is possible that she has decided that the session is over, or she may be testing you to see if you'll give her a treat for not doing anything. She will quickly learn that if she wants a treat, she'll have to do the requested activity.

Sometimes cats become creative and touch the target with different parts of their body. For this initial target-touching exercise, mark the event with a click and a treat only when she touches the target with her nose. As cute as it is for her to reach out with her paw or to head-butt the target, resist the temptation to click and treat for anything other than a nose-to-target touch.

Repetitions are good; they build confidence and they solidify behaviors. After your cat learns the behavior and performs it correctly at least eight out of ten times, add a verbal request.

THREE HANDS WOULD BE NICE

Remember to hold the clicker and the treats with one hand while holding the target with the other. This will help eliminate possible fear responses when the clicker is clicked. Some cats become startled by the click when it's adjacent to or touching the target. The clicker can make the target vibrate if the two are held in the same hand, making touching the target an unpleasant experience for your cat. In addition, it's very easy to accidentally bonk the cat on her sensitive nose if the target is held in the same hand as the clicker, as your movement to click can also move the target.

Add the verbal cue "touch" only after your cat shows she knows the behavior by repeating it correctly eight out of ten times.

Gradually increase the space between your cat's nose and the target until she follows it a short distance.

Decide on one word that you will always use when asking for the behavior—and don't change it! *Touch* makes sense for the target-touching behavior. As you are lowering the target into position near your cat's nose, say the word "touch." As she touches the target, click and then treat. It can take many repetitions until your cat associates the behavior with the word *touch*. Assigning a word to a behavior is important, because eventually you will want her to do behaviors from verbal cues.

After she understands *touch*, make it a little more interesting for both of you by placing the target about ½ to 1 inch farther away from her nose. Again, say "touch" as you lower the target into position, and when she touches that target, simultaneously click and give her a treat. Gradually increase the distance that the target is held from her nose by small increments until she follows the target by taking a few steps.

If she doesn't touch the target, rethink the motivator and the training schedule as previously mentioned. Consider also that you might be asking for too much too soon. Step back to the first nose-to-target exercise and proceed more slowly, increasing the distance from the target to her nose by smaller increments. Another possibility is that she may be done working for the day. Never force her to perform; instead, put the clicker and target away and try again another time, when she is more motivated to work.

Touching the target is a great first behavior because it is simple and helps both you and the cat learn what clicker training is about. This first lesson is also a perfect introduction to the concepts of timing and communicating on a different level with your cat. Touching and following a target is a very useful behavior for modifying other behaviors, such as counter surfing, and for socializing shy kitties.

Second Behavior: Over Here, Please!

The second behavior also uses a prop. The goal is for your cat to stand with all four paws on a specified object after you cue her. She doesn't have to stay yet. She'll learn to stay in chapter 3. A simple placemat is a good general-purpose prop because it can be picked up and put away between sessions, and you can move it to work on the behavior in different areas of your house. Depending on your ultimate goal, a few examples of other common household items that can serve as props are a stool, a small rug, and a litter box or shallow plastic bin turned upside down with a colorful piece of carpet glued on top.

BE CAREFUL WHAT YOU CLICK FOR!

Clicker training is powerful. It is as easy to click and reinforce unwanted behaviors as it is to click and reinforce desired behaviors. Watch your cat's body language when working with her. Don't click and treat if she is showing any signs of anxiety, aggression, or nervousness. Be alert for dilated or constricted pupils, ears held back, fur rippling, vocalizing, tail thumping, and other signs of an unhappy or anxious cat. Clicking while she is expressing these emotional states can reinforce them. Remember, you want to accentuate and reward only the positive.

Use your imagination and consider your ultimate goal. If you want to stop your cat from counter surfing, use a tall stool placed near the counter as a prop. The use of the stool along with clicker training and other behavior-modification methods will help stop the surfing. One reason high stools are perfect for stopping counter surfing activities is because cats sometimes counter surf to be up high. The stool satisfies this need and it also provides a perfect alternative location to

A placemat is a good prop to use for the second behavior because it can be moved throughout the house.

Shaping rewards each incremental step that results in the goal behavior—in this case, standing on the placemat.

hang out other than the counter. You can read more about this in chapter 2.

A placemat or a small rug are effective props for helping to modify and shape a variety of behaviors, including aggression problems, and desensitizing a cat for nail clipping. Placemats and rugs provide versatile default locations for the cat to go to. They can be moved around throughout the house, depending on the circumstances of the behavior problems being addressed.

Behavior challenges can be effectively remedied through the use of props combined with other behavior-modification and management methods. The upside-down litter box with a rug glued on top is fun to use because it looks like a performance podium. Your sweet little kitty will look like a miniature performing tiger. Use your imagination in choosing your prop and don't forget rule number one—make it fun!

Once you've found the perfect prop for your cat, it is time to teach her to stand on it when requested. There are two clicker-training paths—*shaping* and *luring*—that can be used to accomplish this four-paws-on-the-mat behavior. Both methods are important—shaping teaches valuable training skills, and luring jump-starts behaviors.

Method 1: Shaping

Shaping is a very important skill for both cat and cat parent to learn, especially for teaching complex behaviors. The essence of shaping is breaking a complex behavior down into tiny steps and then rewarding the cat for each correct and minute movement that gets the cat closer to the goal behavior. Shaping gradually teaches a behavior by rewarding the cat after each small, successive improvement until the goal behavior is reached. This method takes a little longer to implement, but it builds a stronger behavior and gives you and your cat a sturdy foundation in the language of clicker training.

Start by putting the placemat right next to your cat as a cue. If she investigates it, click and then treat her. Reset by picking up the mat and then cuing her again by putting it down again. This time, if she puts one paw on the mat, click as her paw touches the mat and then treat her. If she ignores the placemat, do not click or treat her; instead, ignore the non-behavior, pick up the placemat, and put it down next to her again. She might decide to comply with your wishes and put two paws down, or she might put one paw down further onto the mat. Click and treat any behavior that takes her closer to the goal behavior of standing with all four paws on the mat, After each click and treat, pick up the mat so that you can cue her again for the behavior. Shaping behaviors can be very subtle, made up of tiny baby steps. At first, even a head glance toward the mat or a paw moved in the right direction might be marked with a click.

NO VERBAL CORRECTIONS

If your cat doesn't understand your cues, don't verbalize negative messages to her about it. Your cat should have fun during these exercises and feel safe to experiment with different behaviors. Verbalizing your disappointment can create a tense situation for the cat. Instead, ignore her and don't click and treat; simply request the behavior again with a cue, clicking and then treating as she performs after being cued.

If your cat does not complete the behavior on request, do not click and treat.

When your cat is standing on the mat, click and toss the treat a short distance away from the placemat, then pick up the mat while she is munching on the treat. Tossing the treat away from the mat forces the cat to move off the mat to eat the treat, allowing you to easily pick up the mat and then give the cue for the behavior again by placing the mat down next to her after she inhales her treat. Cats are smart. Once she understands that she will receive a treat for simply standing on the mat, she will stay put. It makes sense to her to stand on the mat and have treats tossed to her all day long. After all, if she's being treated for just standing on the mat, why should she move off it?

Remember, timing is everything. It is important to click at the very moment the cat takes each baby step. If she doesn't progress, don't click and treat her. And however tempting it may be, do not pick her up or push her in the right direction; this will not accomplish the goal. Be patient, and don't forget that you are now operating in cat time.

Method 2: Luring

The second technique is called *luring*. This is useful when you need immediate results, such as stopping dangerous door-darting. The target and, sometimes, food are used as temporary lures. Because your kitty can now follow a target, you can use it to lead her a short distance to the placemat, after putting the mat next to her. Immediately click and treat her when she is standing with all four paws on the mat. Phase out or stop using luring after the cat correctly repeats the behavior a couple of times. Following the target is not the cue for the mat behavior; the cue is the mat being put

Click and immediately treat your cat when she accomplishes the goal behavior—in this case, standing entirely on the mat.

down on the floor next to her. Most cats only need to be lured to the mat a couple of times. After the cat understands what you are requesting, putting the place mat next to her will be enough of a cue.

It may take a couple of sessions or more until she stands on the placemat when cued. Some cats are *wunderkinder* and pick up on the behavior in only one session. For other cats, it might take a few sessions until they get it. Once the cat stands on the mat, she can be taught to sit, shake hands, and high five, as well as perform other behaviors and parlor tricks.

Going to and standing on the placemat or on another designated object is an important behavior for cats to learn. The mat or stool, depending on the behavior being modified, can act as a default location for the cat to go when working on behavioral challenges that are addressed in the book. Depending on the challenge, the cat's special spot has different functions. As mentioned, the stool is a perfect place for the counter surfer because it is almost at counter height and it becomes more fun and rewarding to sit on a stool than the counter. Door darters can be taught to sit and stay for a length of time on a mat, stool, cat tree, or other location when doors are opened.

Adding Verbal Cues

After your cat has learned to stand on the mat through either luring or shaping, add a verbal cue. Add the verbal cue only after your cat demonstrates that she completely understands the behavior by successfully standing on the mat eight out of ten times after you cue her by putting the mat down next to her. Say the word "mat" or another descriptive word for the object as you are putting the placemat next to her. Don't forget to click when she stands on the designated object and then toss her a treat away from the object she is standing on.

CLICKING FOR *PURRFECT BEHAVIOR*

When your cat does a trick perfectly, or maybe goes above and beyond the call of duty, resist the urge to click her multiple times. Click only once, but then show your appreciation by rewarding her with double the treats and enthusiastic praise. Make sure your cat knows she's the best cat in the whole world.

Eventually you won't have to click every time your cat performs a correct behavior.

A Glimpse into Your Future

Many chapters from now, when you and your cat are thoroughly versed in clicker training and your cat has been performing a behavior perfectly over many days, you won't have to mark the behavior with a click every time she does it right. After awhile, you also won't have to reward her each time with a treat.

The click is used when teaching new behavior, modifying behavior, and, when needed, strengthening behavior (all animals get lazy). After your cat has repeated a behavior correctly over a few days or weeks, responding to your verbal cues each time, you can slowly phase out the click and replace it with a simple *good girl* as she displays the correct behavior.

This process should be gradual. Start by asking her for the behavior, as usual. Then, instead of clicking every time she does it, click four out of five times, but make sure you tell her she's a good girl every time. Gradually increase the amount of times you don't mark the event with the clicker until you are not using the clicker to mark the behavior at all. Don't forget to praise her each time she performs correctly. If she doesn't demonstrate the behavior when cued, go back to clicking until the behavior is solid, and then gradually decrease the clicking again. You may find that you need to occasionally click her to mark the behavior if she starts to get a little lazy, such as not going into a full sit when cued.

Decreasing the frequency of the treat can be handled in a similar way. In clicker-speak, this is referred to as a *variable schedule of reinforcement.* Instead of giving her a treat every time she successfully completes the behavior when cued, randomly give her treats. Start by treating her only four out of five times, then gradually decrease the frequency of the treats until you are treating her for

After the cat is well versed in a behavior, the frequency she receives treat rewards can be decreased.

two out of five correct repetitions. You will know you're rushing the process if the cat doesn't exhibit the behavior on request anymore or if she is taking longer than usual to complete the task. If that happens, go back and click and treat her each time she does the correct behavior. Eventually, you can slowly decrease the rewards again, but make sure you reward the cat enough times to make it worth her while. Never stop the rewards completely; you probably wouldn't work long for free, and neither will your cat.

Consistency is important. Do your best to schedule clicker training sessions every day.

Some behaviors will always need to be reinforced by clicking and treating. One example is when clicker training is used to help relax and condition the cat for medical procedures. Your cat not only needs to be treated each time, but the treat has to be something that she *highly* covets.

Do It!

In order to change unappreciated behavior successfully, cats should be clicker-trained every day. Multiple short sessions are the most effective when first starting to clicker-train because a cat's attention can wander early on in the process. The length of the sessions will increase as the cat learns and enjoys the process. Optimally, clicker sessions should occur more than once a day. Like anything else, the more you practice, the better you'll become. Because cats thrive on consistency, try to have at least one of the sessions at the same time every day. Modern life sometimes makes it impossible to be consistent, but do the best you can do.

Clicker training is powerful! The few basic techniques mentioned in this chapter, combined with the replacement activities and changes to the environment discussed in the following chapters, are the building blocks that will help you eliminate unappreciated cat behavior while strengthening the essential cat–human bond. The following chapters each address a specific problem behavior and the clicker-training methods that you can use to curb it.

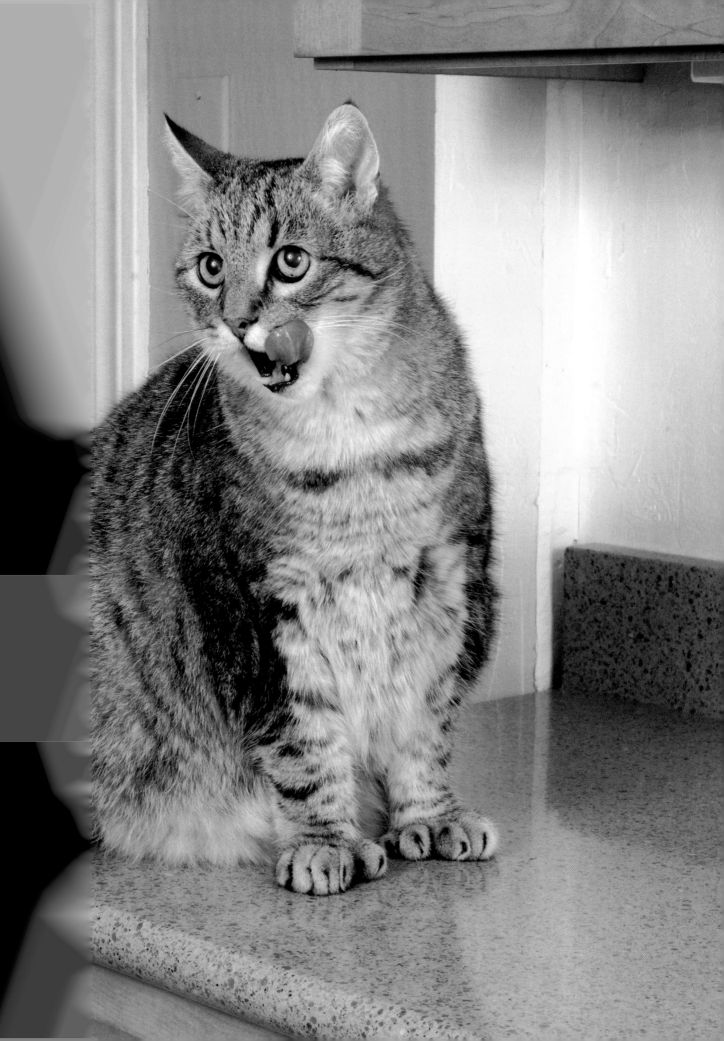

The Counter Surfer

Counter surfing, keyboard walking, and table dancing are common cat behaviors that leave people frustrated and upset. Sautéing dinner with one hand while attempting to keep the cat from jumping up on the stove with the other is annoying and can be dangerous for cat and human alike. In efforts to stop these behaviors, many methods have been used with varying degrees of success. These methods range from punishment to coddling, and the majority of them are not successful because they do not address the underlying cause of the behavior.

Squirt bottles, loud noises, products that shock, cans of air that hiss, and yelling are a few of the generally ineffective aversive methods used in attempts to train cats to stop surfing.

THE COUNTER-SURFING SOLUTIONS TOOL KIT

- **Primary reinforcer** (treats)
- **Secondary reinforcer** (clicker)
- **Target** (pencil or chopstick)
- **Plastic placemats**
- **Wide double-sided tape** (you can find this in a pet-supply store)
- **Alternative locations** (cat tree, window perch, and/or tall stool)

That being said, note that some of these aversive tools, such as squirt bottles, can be effective in saving a cat's life. A squirt from a squirt bottle can stop a cat from jumping up on the stove in the moment. Squirt bottles and other aversive materials don't train cats to stop displaying a behavior in the long term, but they can save lives when used appropriately.

Often, the use of aversive tools such as shock mats and hissing cans results in cats escalating their unwanted behavior or exhibiting other undesirable behavior. These types of products can also frighten cats, causing them to respond with redirected aggression such as biting or hissing at the nearest animal or human. Additionally, using punishment can damage the cat–human bond, causing cats to be afraid and insecure around their human companions. Unfortunately, cats often associate the punishment with the punisher.

Clicker training, when used with management, is a fun and frustration-free way to train cats to keep off of counters, computer keyboards, and other surfaces without using fear tactics or punishment. Added benefits are that cats and their people have fun together and strengthen the bonds between them.

Clicker training, when combined with management, can help train cats to stay off of counters.

Let's Play Detective

In order to successfully modify behavior, it's important to determine the underlying cause and then manage, modify, or eliminate the triggers of the unappreciated behavior. It is also crucial to give the cat something more fun to do in exchange. So, let's put our detective hats on, go into sleuth mode, and figure out the motivation for surfing. Determining the cause is essential because solutions vary depending on what triggered the behavior. Some of the reasons for counter surfing are obvious; others call for in-depth investigation.

Food is a primary and obvious motivator for counter surfing. Perhaps there is one little shred of last night's dinner, a small morsel that escaped the sponge.

Or maybe the dishes are still sitting in the sink and the leftovers are waiting for a ride to the refrigerator. Garbage disposals typically harbor vestiges of meals. Don't forget that cats have very developed noses and can smell food that we can't even begin to detect. If your cat is motivated by food, she is a Foodie. Food can definitely be a primary reason for counter surfing, but usually there are additional reasons.

Food is a major trigger for counter surfing. Make sure to clean up the counters and wash the dishes.

Most cats enjoy being up high. Height is one way that cats display status to both animal and human companions. Counters are also perfect locations from which to see everything going on in the kitchen, including who comes and goes. Many cats enjoy communing at eye level with their people. Counters provide the perfect opportunity for social interaction and networking with their favorite humans. And if next to a window, counters provide wonderful views of neighborhood activities. A cat who enjoys these activities is a Networker.

Being safe and secure are prime directives for all cats, though some cats are more fearful than others. Sitting on a counter will allow these Safety Seekers to keep an eye on other animal residents around whom she may feel uncomfortable. If there is a dog in the home, a countertop provides a safe haven out of his reach. Cats can also feel insecure around young toddlers who might chase and annoy them. Again, an easy escape is to [jum]p onto the counter.

[It's] common for people to unknow[ingly r]einforce, refine, and encourage [the c]at's surfing behavior by engag[ing wi]th the cat while she's up on the [count]er. Because most cats enjoy inter[acting] with their favorite people, pick[ing th]em up, talking to them, or yelling [at the]m can reinforce counter surfing. [Coun]ter surfing can then become a fun [and] attention-getting activity for cats.

WHY COUNTER

Card For A Free Guide!

[Car]d and receive a *FREE* Guide to Flea & Tick Prevention.
(While supplies last)

[p]urchasing one of BowTie's exceptional books. We are
[intere]sted in any comments you may have on your *Naughty*
[...]se and thank you for your time.

[...]receive special e-mail promotions from carefully selected third parties.

☐ 19-25   ☐ 26-45   ☐ 46-55   ☐ Over 55

State_____

[inte]rest to you?

☐ Dogs   ☐ Birds   ☐ Critters   ☐ Farming/Gardening   ☐ Green Living

[addr]ess, visit bowtiepress.com

Some attention-seeking cats escalate the behavior by jumping repeatedly onto counters or knocking items off the counter. They develop it into a game that only they enjoy. If this sounds like your cat, you have an Attention Seeker.

As you can see, there are many reasons why a cat may surf. Cats are complex creatures, and they usually have more than one valid and reasonable motivation for counter surfing—valid and reasonable to the cat, anyway.

The Management Side of Counter Surfing

If the primary motivation for your Foodie's surfing activities is the remnants of lunch on the counter or the dishes in the sink, then the first items on your agenda are to wash the dishes, scrub the sink, and put away any food. Convincing the kids to put their dishes in the dishwasher and your spouse to wipe down the counter might be a bigger challenge than convincing the cat not to use the counter as her own personal runway, but everyone in the household needs to do his or her part.

If your Safety Seeker is hanging out on the counter because it provides a safe haven away from other resident animals or young children, buy or build one or two tall cat trees and put them in the rooms where she's counter surfing. Your

A tall stool placed next to the counter provides an alternative location for the cat to sit.

cat will be eternally grateful if you position one next to a secure window. Sturdy shelves and window perches that are located out of the reach of other animals and youngsters can also provide safe areas for your cat. These cat trees and perches need to be high enough so that they are child- and dog-free zones. Managing the situation by keeping the other resident animals away from your cat will also help keep her safe and happy.

The Networker loves to be up high. She needs a tall stool or a comfortable shelf, window perch, or cat tree with shelves at different levels near the counter on which she surfs. If there's a window nearby, she'll appreciate sitting on a tall cat tree so that she can check out the neighborhood.

Attention Seekers also need tall stools. They need to be managed and worked with differently than Foodies, Safety Seekers, and Networkers because some of the management techniques can reinforce their attention-seeking behaviors; this is explained in more detail later in the chapter.

Persuasive Change

Next on the agenda is to make the counter an uncomfortable place for your cat to hang out while simultaneously providing an acceptable place to sit that satisfies your cat's surfing urges. Double-sided tape is usually persuasive, as most cats do not like the feel of it. Buy cheap plastic placemats, cut and size them if needed, and adhere the tape to one side of them. Place the mats, sticky-side up, on the counters. Placing obstacles on the counter will also make counters and other surfaces hard to navigate.

Make the counters undesirable places to be by putting on them placemats covered with double sided tape.

When making counters unattractive to the cat, be sure to provide another location that fulfills her reasons for counter surfing. Never take something away or make something unavailable without replacing it with something else that is more appealing and fun. In order to successfully change an unwanted behavior, the cat needs a new activity that she enjoys more than the old one. Tall kitchen chairs or bar stools are ideal for this, as they are fairly close in height to counters or tables. The best location for the stool is near the counter or table that the cat's been surfing on. Other alternative places for the cat to sit include window perches and 5- to 6-foot-tall cat trees.

TWO-SIDED SOLUTION

In addition to management, the causes of the surfing behavior need to be modified and the cat needs to be given something else to do. In order to be successful, all are necessary. When modifying or eliminating the underlying reasons for the behavior, it is important to have another activity that is more fun and motivating than the original, unappreciated behavior. Clicker training is perfect for this. When practiced on a consistent basis, clicker training is fun and refocuses the cat on something more inspiring. It's kind of like replacement therapy for cats.

The Clicker and Counter Surfing

Now that everything is in place, you can convince your cat that it's more fun to be on her own personal stool near the counter or on a window perch than to be on a surface that is now sticky and cluttered. Remember, Attention Seekers who counter surf need to be trained differently than those cats who have other reasons for surfing, but regardless of your cat's motivation for counter surfing, don't yell at her or attempt to stare her down, pet her, or squirt her with water.

Before teaching cats not to counter surf, you need to provide a solid basis in clicker training.

You need to establish a communication system and start sending the message to your errant kitty that you prefer her on the stool instead of dancing on the countertops. For the Foodie, start delivering your message by unceremoniously picking her up and immediately putting her on the floor when she's attempting to navigate the sticky counter. This method usually isn't effective with the Attention Seeker; she will interpret this as an invitation to interact and may respond by immediately bouncing back up on the counter. Even though the interaction might be brief, it can become a game for the cat and escalate into frustration for the chosen human.

Clicker training, when used with management, helps convince cats that there are other places that are more fun to hang out than on the counters. Before starting, all of the players need to have a solid foundation in the clicker-training basics covered in chapter 1. The clicker needs to be paired with the primary motivator, and both the cat and her trainer have to be well versed in target and mat training before attempting to click away counter-surfing activities.

Clicker Training the Foodies, Networkers, and Safety Seekers

If your cat is anything but an Attention Seeker, quickly remove her from the counter and place her on the floor. As soon as she is on the floor, use the target as a cue, tapping it on the stool a few times. If your cat's targeting skills are solid, she will jump up onto the stool. As she jumps on the stool, click and then treat her. For those cats who don't respond to the tapping cue, use the target as a lure, positioning it so that she follows it and finally jumps up onto the stool. If that doesn't work, practice your targeting skills and check the "yum factor" of your motivator. Your motivator needs to be *very* motivating. I hesitate to mention this, but when the situation is dire and you want an immediate result, you can cheat on the first couple of repetitions by putting tuna juice, or something else that rocks your cat's socks, on the end of the target. When using food lures, phase

Tap the target a couple of times on the stool to cue your cat to jump onto the stool.

them out as soon as possible. Remember, food is not the cue; food is the primary reinforcer for doing the job right.

Once your cat is successful at jumping up onto the stool immediately after being cued with the target, and she repeats the behavior perfectly a few times in a row, you can phase out the use of the target by tapping your finger on the stool to cue her to jump up. Many repetitions and sessions down the road, you will be able to simply point to the stool and give a verbal cue.

THE DANGERS OF FOOD LURES

As a general rule, I do not recommend using food-laced targets for luring cats. The use of lures should be minimal and only when the problem behavior is dangerous and the cat needs to be jump-started on a replacement behavior right away. When using food lures, make sure to phase out their use after the second or third repetition. Cats, like all animals, are opportunists and will confuse the lure with the treat and start to expect the treat before the behavior and won't perform the behavior. This is the feline equivalent of putting the cart before the horse.

Again, cats are smart. Some smarty-cats figure out very quickly that after they jump up onto the counter, they will be removed and then rewarded for jumping onto the stool. These cats respond by bouncing back up onto the counter right after they've inhaled their treats. This is a variation on the attention-seeking personality. You need to always be one step ahead. When you suspect that your cat is playing this game, work with her exactly as you would work with an Attention Seeker (see the following section).

Clicker Training the Attention Seeker

The Attention Seeker can be easily identified. She is the cat who frequently demands attention from her favorite person through tactics that can be annoying. These tactics can include in-your-face meowing or pawing, knocking objects off of tables, bouncing up onto forbidden surfaces, and other repetitive behaviors that result in what the cat wants: constant interaction with her human companion.

In addition to making the countertops unpleasant places to hang out, you need to ignore the Attention Seeker.

The Attention Seeker will need a slightly different approach than the other personality types when she is up on the counter because putting her down on the floor can cause what I call the *yo-yo* effect—constantly bouncing back up, ready for more fun. Instead of placing the Attention Seeker on the floor, do the opposite. Ignore the counter-dancing behavior by walking away or turning your back on the errant cat. Ignoring the behavior also means not having a discussion with your cat or mouthing expletives. When your attention-seeking cat is on the counter, she needs to be invisible to you.

In addition to ignoring the surfing, practice the fine art of *capturing behavior.* It's simple: click and then treat when your cat finally steps or jumps onto the stool. Capturing behavior means reinforcing a behavior when it occurs naturally without the cat being prompted or cued. Because the counters will be inconvenient and covered with double-sided tape, the comfortable, uncluttered stool will become very appealing. After you click, toss the treat on the floor. You want the cat to jump down off the stool to get the treat, thereby automatically resetting the exercise.

LEARNING IN THE TRENCHES

I share my life with Bengals and Savannahs. These are highly intelligent and active cats. Without a doubt, they are stereotypical Attention Seekers. Sometimes it's hard to know who is training whom. Living with highly intelligent cats means thinking out of the box in addition to exploring all possible clicker solutions for changing unwanted behaviors.

My cats can go anywhere in my house, except on the stove. When I began training them to not jump up on the stove, I followed the standard protocol, placing placemats stuck with double-sided tape on the stove. When the cats jumped up, I would remove them from the stove, quickly depositing them on the floor without so much as a look or a word. Contrary to what was supposed to happen, the stove perching escalated. Being the little Attention Seekers they are, they quickly decided that this was a fun game and immediately yo-yoed back up onto the stove, looking for more action and interaction. My actions of picking them up and putting them on the floor—however brief—reinforced the stove-cruising behavior because I was interacting with them, which was what they wanted.

Through trial and error, I discovered that the clicker training technique of *capturing* the behavior I wanted was very effective in training my Attention Seekers to stay off the stove. Capturing a behavior means first paying close attention to what the cat is doing. When she naturally does a desired behavior without being prompted, reinforce the behavior by clicking while she's engaged in the approved behavior and then immediately rewarding her with a treat. In my case, when my cats jumped onto or stood on the stools, they were immediately reinforced with a click and rewarded with a small piece of dehydrated chicken.

Universal Clicking for Surfers

No matter what your cat's motivations for surfing are, click as she touches or stands on the stool. Immediately after the click, treat her, throwing the treat on the floor so that she has to jump off the stool to eat it. Repeat the request, tapping the target on the stool again. Every time she jumps onto the stool, click and treat her. When your cat jumps up on the counter; repeat the whole cycle either by putting the Foodie, Networker, or Safety Seeker on the floor or by ignoring the Attention Seeker and capturing the right

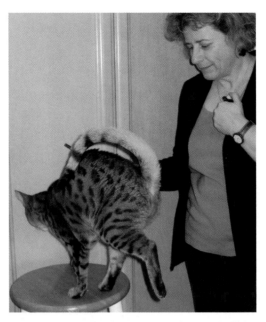

As soon as your cat jumps up on the stool, click her and then immediately treat her.

behavior. Soon your cat will understand that the stool is a much nicer place to sit than the sticky, cluttered counter. An added benefit is that your cat is exercising.

EXTINCTION BURSTS

Cats, as well as other species, can exhibit what is called in clicker-speak *extinction bursts* when they are initially being trained out of a behavior. The behavior you are trying to stop, or extinguish, temporarily becomes stronger. Don't be surprised if your cat initially starts frequenting the counters more often and getting in your face or meowing while up there. The behavior can escalate before it fades away and finally stops. The Attention Seeker is infamous for this. The behavior will stop once the cat realizes that she is not being reinforced or rewarded for it.

Adding the Verbal Cue

After your cat prefers the stool to the counter, hang a verbal cue on the behavior. You will know that she understands what you are asking of her when she jumps onto the stool at least eight out of ten times instead of jumping up on the counter. Associate the verbal cue with the behavior by saying "up" as you tap the stool with the target. Any word will work as long as it's used consistently for the same behavior. Don't forget to click every time she lands on the stool, and then follow the click with a treat tossed on the floor.

Eventually, after many repetitions in separate sessions, you will be able to gradually phase out the use of the target or your tapping finger and rely on the verbal cue alone. After a while, you can also reward her on a variable schedule of reinforcement, as explained in chapter 1.

Sit

Once your cat has mastered hanging out on the designated stool, you can teach her to sit on command. This is a fairly easy behavior to teach, and one that you can impress your friends with.

Work with her when she's up on her stool. Hold either the target, one finger, or a treat slightly above her head and in front of her face so that your cat can see it. The usual response that a cat gives to the target (or your finger) or lure is to reach for it by extending her nose

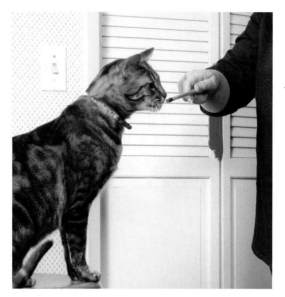

Teaching your cat to sit on her designated stool is fun and effective for stopping her counter surfing.

up toward it. Typically, as she reaches for it, she will sit. At the exact second that her little derrière touches the stool, click and follow with the treat. Timing is crucial. You want to mark the event by clicking just as her rear end touches the stool. Don't click after or before she sits. If you use a food lure to jump-start the behavior, stop using it after a couple of repetitions, replacing it with your finger and then finally with a verbal cue.

After she thoroughly learns the behavior, performing it correctly eight out of ten times, add a verbal cue. Not surprisingly, the verbal cue is the word *sit*. Say "sit" as you use your finger or target, cuing her to sit. Of course, click and treat her for her performance. Make sure she knows she's the smartest cat in the world.

IMPRESS THE NEIGHBORS

Impress your friends and neighbors by teaching your cats some extraordinary bar-stool tricks such as staying, shaking hands, jumping between stools and through hoops, turning around, and sitting pretty, all while on the stool. Use your imagination, but teach only safe and natural behaviors. Instructions for some of these behaviors can be found in chapter 9.

Case Study: Counter Surfing

SITUATION: Red and Swirl, two rambunctious eleven-month-old orange male cats, loved to spend their evenings in the kitchen. Their favorite pastimes were counter surfing and disposal diving. Their human companions, Robert and Sue, adored the two cats, but they also loved to keep an immaculate home and did not appreciate the cats' behavior. After their long days at work, Rob and Sue simply wanted to prepare and eat their dinner and have a quiet, relaxing evening.

Rob and Sue have always kept consistent schedules. Sue would feed the cats at 6:00 p.m. and then start preparing dinner at 6:30. The couple always ate at 7:30. The cats had their own schedules and agendas, however. The two Foodies would inhale their dinner, and then bounce up on the counters and into the sink, scrounging and stealing food at 6:35, just as Sue was preparing dinner.

The couple tried to stop the counter surfing by using squirt bottles, shock mats, and motion-activated cans of air that hiss. Nothing worked. They finally reached the end of their rope when Red bit Sue severely after being frightened by the noise of hissing air when he jumped up onto the sink. Sue became afraid of Red, and the two cats became frightened of both Rob and Sue.

ASSESSMENT: Red and Swirl were primarily surfing and disposal diving because they are Foodies; the intriguing food scraps on the counter were irresistible to them. It didn't help that Sue, a gourmet cook, always had a smorgasbord of delights pleasingly arranged on the counter. Additionally, Rob and Sue were reinforcing the behavior by extensively interacting with the cats when they were up on the counter. Because the two cats were left alone all day, they would do anything for attention from their favorite people when they finally came home. Unfortunately, because of the aversive techniques that Rob and Sue used, the cat–human bond deteriorated.

RECOMMENDATIONS: I recommended a combination of management and clicker training and I banned the squirt bottles, hissing cans, and shock mats from the house.

Rob and Sue rearranged their schedules to incorporate quality time with the cats, playing with them for ten minutes before giving the cats their dinner. They also provided each cat with his own bar stool, located near the counter. Sue then cut three plastic placemats in half, covered them with double-sided tape and positioned them strategically on the counters, making the countertops unpleasant areas to navigate. Swirl was the first cat to test the waters. He leaped up on the counter, found it irksome, and promptly jumped down. Sue immediately tapped the target on the stool once. Swirl bounded up, and Sue clicked him and threw the treat on the floor. Red then decided to jump up on the counter, this time where Sue was preparing food. Sue picked him up and quickly deposited him on the floor without comment. She then tapped the stool, and Red responded by leaping up onto the stool. Sue clicked and treated him just like she had done with Swirl.

It took patience and a bit of an extinction burst, but the cats finally understood what was expected of them. Everyone in the household, cats and people alike, found that they really enjoyed clicker training. An added benefit was that clicker training helped rebuild the trust and strengthen the cat–human bond that had been weakened by the aversive techniques.

The motivation to surf was further diminished by Sue and Rob keeping the counters food-free between meals. After dinner, Sue made sure that she put all of the dishes in the dishwasher, wiped down the counters, and cleaned the sink.

Within a few weeks, Red and Swirl began to hang out on the stools whenever Sue started to prepare the evening meal. She continued to reward them for their good behavior, and she eventually trained them to stay, shake hands, and sit pretty.

CHAPTER 3

Dangerous Door Darting

How many times have you struggled to open the door while carrying heavy bags of groceries and simultaneously trying to block your Indy 500 racing cat from darting out the door? Or maybe you have an opportunistic cat who lives for the chance to make a mad dash through any door that's open for more than a fraction of a second.

Don't take this behavior lightly; door darting can be fatal. Frequently, cats who rush doors meet unfortunate ends by running into traffic or disappearing forever. You can greatly decrease the odds of this occurring by teaching your cat to stay in one location when doors are open.

DOOR-DARTING SOLUTIONS TOOL KIT

- **Primary reinforcer** (treats)
- **Secondary reinforcer** (clicker)
- **Target** (pencil)
- **Alternative locations** (cat tree, kitchen stool, or tall chair)
- **Environmental enrichment** (interactive toys)

Clicker training can teach cats to sit and stay on cue when doors are opened.

Training your cat to stay on request is also very useful kitchen etiquette. It helps ensure that whiskers and tails aren't singed, that bowls aren't licked, and that cooks can move freely through the kitchen without worrying about tripping over the cat. Teaching a cat to stay is also very handy for stopping overzealous cats from begging or mobbing their people for food.

You can stop door darting by teaching the cat alternative behaviors that are more rewarding than rushing doors. In order to convince your cat that staying in a designated spot is fun, you'll use a combination of management and clicker training and make sure that the behavior you are asking for is much more fun than the behavior that is being replaced.

Keep in mind that even the best-trained cats can have lapses, so it's important to close doors and be vigilant about situations that might result in the cat making a mad dash for the door.

BE SAFE: MICROCHIP YOUR CATS

Whether your cat is a door darter or perfectly happy sleeping on the couch, situations can occur that are completely out of your control. Be prepared and make sure that your cats are microchipped, and don't forget to register your cat with the microchipping company.

Microchips are small chips that contain vital information about the cat, including the owners' contact information and the veterinarian's information. The cat's information is registered with a microchipping company. If the cat is lost and then found, the cat can be scanned by a reader, the microchip company contacted, and the cat's information retrieved to reunite her with her people. A microchip is embedded by a veterinarian under the skin located on the back of the cat's neck.

The Management Side of Door Darting

In addition to using clicker training to teach your door darter to stay, you will need to make a few changes so that the inside of your house is more appealing and exciting than the outside. You won't have to turn your home into a kitty Disneyland, but there are some human-furniture rearrangements and cat-furniture additions that will help make the environment more cat-centric. Putting your cat on a consistent schedule for feeding, clicker training, play, and other interactions that she enjoys will also help convince her that being inside is more fascinating than roaming around outside.

Provide your little door darter with tall furniture that she can climb on and view her world from. You can make your own furniture, buy furniture, or be innovative and use whatever you have on hand to create high places for your cat to hang out. Ideally, cat furniture should be sturdy and at least 5 feet tall, constructed with wide shelves and a wide base. The wide base will prevent active cats from accidentally pulling it over when bounding up it. The shelves should be configured so that one cat can't be trapped by other resident cats—in other words, shelves should not be located one directly under the other. Multiple routes up and down the cat tree need to be provided either by the configuration of the shelves or by other pieces of furniture placed next to it. Good locations for tall cat furniture are areas that your cat already likes to hang out in. Usually these are rooms where her favorite people spend the most time.

FROM THE WILD TO THE WARM

Statistics show that cats live longer and healthier lives when they are always kept indoors. Cats who are allowed outside are at risk for being stolen, contracting parasites, and dying prematurely from disease, poisoning, or encounters with dogs, other cats, wild animals, or cars.

Regular play and environmental enrichment will help keep cats stimulated and happy.

There is some very creative cat furniture on the market. Some manufacturers use real tree limbs when constructing their cat furniture; others use alternative materials, such as composites, plastics, or metal combined with stiff fabrics and other sturdy material for their trees. Wide wall-mounted shelves, tall bookcases, and window perches can also provide your cat the vertical territory and the height she needs.

WATCH THOSE DOGGY DOORS

Door darters are not only notorious for dashing out slightly open windows and doors, but they are also adept at taking advantage of doggy doors. Many cats are very skilled at opening them; others wait for their companion dog to let himself out and then race between his legs and...zip—they're gone!

Interactive toys that keep your cats busy are also a must. Puzzle boxes and ball-and-track toys are a couple of popular options. Brown paper bags with their handles cut off (for safety) or cardboard boxes can also provide entertainment for your little door darter. Tunnels and cat hideouts are also available; some have many compartments for exploring. And don't forget the simple things—many cats love chasing after little pieces of wadded-up paper. There are lots of creative and fun toys to choose from. You can chase the boredom blues away by rotating the toys every week or so. Use your imagination, but make sure that any toys you make or buy are safe for the cat.

There are many creative cat furniture solutions available that are both fun for the cat and aesthetically pleasing.

Food can become a challenging and enjoyable event for your cat. If you feed your cat dry food, consider putting the food in a treat ball instead of a bowl. A treat ball is a hard, hollow ball with holes in it. You place dry food or treats in the ball, and in order for your cat to access the food, she will have to roll the ball around to make the pieces of food drop out. You may find that you have to show her how to use it at first. If you spend lots of time away from your cat, you may want to consider a treat ball that records your voice. Every time your cat rolls it around, she will hear you telling her what a wonderful, perfect cat she is.

Some of my favorites include puzzle toys originally made for dogs; they make cats work a little for their treats. One toy has separate compartments that are covered by sliders. In order for the cat to access the food, she has to move the sliders away from the compartments. Another one is made up of hollowed-out plastic dog-bone shapes, positioned on top of each other. The cat has to spin each dog bone in order to reach the food.

Fishing pole toys are fun and entertaining for both the cat and her favorite person.

This puzzle toy makes the cat work for her food. She has to spin the plastic bones in order to access the treats.

Regular scheduled interaction with your cat is mandatory for keeping her content to stay indoors. Use toys to play with her at the same times every day. Ideal play times are right before meals. Give her something delicious to eat immediately after each play session. Consider having daily treasure hunts for your little one just before bed. Hide small pieces of treats or regular dry food in your cat's toys, on her cat furniture or shelves, or in other locations. She will look forward to the game and to interacting with you. If your cat loves to be groomed, have grooming sessions with her every day. Many cats love and need quality lap and cuddle time with their favorite humans. Clicker training should also be done on a schedule.

A SPECIAL TREAT

Cool off your cats on hot summer days using homemade broth ice cubes. Make your own chicken, beef, or other preferred meat broth and freeze it in ice-cube trays. Since most spices are toxic for cats, make sure that there are no spices, including garlic and/or onion, in the broth that you use for the broth cubes. After the broth cubes are frozen, either float one in your cat's water bowl or put one in a large dish for her to bat around and enjoy. Frozen broth ice cubes will keep both you and your cat entertained.

If your cat loves to be groomed, schedule grooming sessions with her around the same time every day.

Click the Door Darter

Cats have mastered the art of being patient. Patience helps ensure a successful hunt. Clicker training is a wonderful way to efficiently capture and reward this natural waiting behavior. It can help build the behavior so that your cat will stay put even if there are a thousand distractions around her and every door in the house is open.

Teaching your cat to stay has its foundations in previously learned behaviors. Staying for duration (for a specified amount of time) and staying during distracting moments (such as a door being opened or dinner being placed on the table) build on both the clicker-trained behaviors of going to a specified location in chapter 1 and the

Before you teach your cat to stay, she will need to be able to sit when verbally cued.

sit that was taught to curb counter surfing in chapter 2. Before she can learn to stay, your cat needs to know how to sit on request. She will also need specific areas designated for her to sit. These cat-centric areas should be stools, chairs, trees, or shelves that give her enough room to sit comfortably for a length of time, and they should be located in several different rooms of the house.

Training systems such as 300 Peck Pigeon can be used to train your cat to stay for set lengths of time and during distractions.

Duration

After your cat has learned to sit and isn't yo-yoing on and off the stool, you can use a couple of systems to gradually increase the duration of time for which she sits. A training technique developed by Alexandra Kurland called 300 Peck Pigeon helps build up duration and is very useful for breaking through

CATS AS INDIVIDUALS

All cat lovers know that every cat is an individual, each with her own personality. It's important to keep that in mind when modifying behavior. Working with cats is a dynamic process. Some cats can be easily distracted and may need the criteria raised or another challenge added, while others are little troopers, willing to work with one behavior for an extended period of time before going to another. Still others may need shorter sessions given on a more frequent basis.

Cats are very intelligent, and they learn quickly. When working with door darters, two distinct criteria need to be worked with: the duration of the stay and staying amidst distractions. You may find that you have to adjust the way you train your cat—training first for duration and then quickly adding a few distractions, or giving your cat a more solid foundation in staying for a length of time before adding distractions. You want to train in a way that will ensure success for the cat. It's all about the cat's success.

plateaus. Or you can vary the approach, clicking for duration and for staying during distractions. Remember, you want to set your cat up for success.

Start by asking your door darter to sit on her designated spot. Do not click or reward her for the *sit* behavior. Instead, after she sits, say the words "one Savannah" silently to yourself and then click and treat her. *One Savannah* equals one second in time. Click and treat the cat only if she quietly stays for the whole second. When treating her, put the treat in front of her so it's easy for her to reach from where she is sitting. You can add a hand cue in the beginning of the behavior by facing your palm toward her with your fingers pointing up. Don't be frustrated, as it may take a few tries until she understands what you are asking of her.

If she moves or jumps down, reset the behavior cycle by requesting that she sit on her stool again. While she is sitting, again silently say "one Savannah" and click and treat her if she sits for the whole second. If she is successful, restart the count while she is waiting patiently, asking for a longer stay by saying "one Savannah, two Savannahs." Click and treat her after she sits and waits the obligatory two seconds. Is she still waiting politely? Restart the count, extending the length once again by counting to yourself up to three seconds. Click and treat her if she stays the whole *three Savannahs*. Do not click her if she starts to move out of position before you've completed your count. If she does move out of

Request that your cat sit. Gradually extend the length of the stay with clicks and treats.

position, start over from the beginning, starting at one second and increasing the count again, until she stays for the equivalent of three seconds, and then click and treat. Restart the count, but this time increase the count to four seconds. Once she can sit and stay on cue for five seconds, eight out of ten times, add a verbal cue. Request the behavior by saying "stay" out loud after she sits. You can repeat the verbal cue a couple of times during lengthy counts.

Congratulate yourself and your cat, because your cat is now responding correctly to two consecutive behavior requests—*sit* and *stay*—and is being acknowledged for it only after completing the second behavior. Combining behaviors like this is called *chaining.*

300 PECK PIGEON

300 Peck Pigeon is a technique that is very useful for building time into a behavior. Alexandra Kurland, a horse trainer, first developed the 300 Peck Pigeon technique. Alexandra says the following about 300 Peck Pigeon: "The training strategy was based on pigeon studies where the researchers were looking at variable reinforcement schedules. When the reinforcement schedules were built slowly and systematically, the researchers could get the pigeons to peck a bar three hundred times for one reinforcement— hence the name." Alexandra Kurland treated the 300-peck duration as the gold standard for building long duration into behavior.

Plateaus

Let's say that your cat is very successful at staying for five seconds without leaping off her chair. But before you reach six seconds, she's off of the chair and cruising around the kitchen. No matter how many times you reset the count, your cat is propelling herself off of the chair just before reaching six seconds. She may

have reached a learning plateau, and 300 Peck Pigeon is a good technique for helping to break through plateaus.

Give your cat the cue to jump on the stool and sit. Then request a *stay*, restarting the count at *one Savannah* and then increasing the count. If she jumps off of the stool at an earlier count, such as four seconds, reset her on the stool, and begin the count again. Click and treat her only when she stays for the six seconds.

To illustrate how 300 Peck Pigeon works in this case, let's say that your cat stays for five seconds without any problems, but is having a challenge with six seconds. The following is how you would help your

Alexandra Kurland's 300 Peck Pigeon technique works well for overcoming learning plateaus.

cat overcome the plateau through 300 Peck Pigeon:

- Start by giving your cat the cue to jump up on the stool, sit, and then stay. Then start the count: *One Savannah, two Savannahs, three Savannahs, four Savannahs, five Savannahs*, and the cat jumps off the stool.
- Reset the behavior by cuing her first to sit on the stool and then to stay.
- *One Savannah, two Savannahs, three Savannahs*, and the cat jumps off the stool to check out a fly.
- Reset the behavior by cuing her first to sit on the stool and then to stay.
- *One Savannah, two Savannahs, three Savannahs, four Savannahs, five Savannahs, six Savannahs*. Click and treat the cat where she is sitting. Note that she only earns a click and treat when she stays for the full count.

Every cat is different, and if your cat seems to be stuck and not breaking through the plateau using the 300 Peck Pigeon technique, then try a variation. It's important to set up your cat for success, and that may mean changing your strategy. One variation involves clicking and treating your cat at a lower count when she has a higher level of success. For instance, if your cat has consistently stayed for four seconds, but breaks before six seconds, click her at three seconds and then gradually increase the count. The following is an example of a variation that illustrates breaking through a learning plateau of five seconds:

- *One Savannah, two Savannahs, three Savannahs, four Savannahs, five Savannahs,* and the cat jumps off the stool.
- Reset the behavior by cuing her first to sit on the stool and then to stay.
- *One Savannah, two Savannahs, three Savannahs,* then click and treat the cat where she is sitting.
- Restart the count.
- *One Savannah, two Savannahs, three Savannahs, four Savannahs,* then click and treat the cat where she is sitting.
- Restart the count.
- *One Savannah, two Savannahs, three Savannahs, four Savannahs, five Savannahs,* then click and treat the cat where she is sitting.
- Restart the count.
- *One Savannah, two Savannahs, three Savannahs, four Savannahs, five Savannahs, six Savannahs,* then click and treat the cat where she is sitting.

BABY STEPS

Think in baby steps; if the cat still isn't catching on, you might be asking too much too fast. Don't expect her to perfect the *stay* in one session. Every cat is different, and some take longer than others. Set your mental clock to "cat time" and proceed at your cat's desired pace. Also pay attention to when you're clicking. You may be clicking too slow or too fast, event-marking at the wrong time, or confusing the cat by clicking conflicting behaviors. Maybe the sessions are too long, and your cat works best with short sessions.

Another consideration is that your time increments may be too long. Instead of waiting for one full second, decrease the time you are asking her to stay. Say to yourself "one" instead of "one Savannah" and click and treat her if she stays. Gradually increase the count, at first using only numbers, and gradually working up to a full-second count.

You might also reevaluate your treat's appeal. The treat might not be motivating enough. Cats change their minds; what was originally a favorite treat can quickly become yesterday's news.

Another variation on the technique is clicking for multiple successes at the same count. So, for example, if your cat is successful at staying for six seconds, instead of increasing to seven seconds, repeat the six-second success, thereby reinforcing and strengthening the six-second stay before increasing the time by one second. Remember, the goal is for your cat to succeed at staying for a set amount of time. Your training strategy needs to be flexible enough to allow for variation in order to ensure her success.

Distractions

Because you want your cat to sit and stay when doors are opened, meals are cooked, and other activities are occurring, you need to add low-level distractions into the extended *stay* behavior. Low-level distractions can begin when your cat has a good grasp on sitting for a set length of time. Start working with distractions by taking one step back while inviting your cat to stay. Click and treat her when she stays put. Practice also by taking a step to the right or left as she is staying. Gradually extend the distance between the two of you, always coming back to click and treat her when she remains in a *stay* position. If she jumps down or moves away, don't click and treat her. Reinforce the desired behavior; ignore the unwanted behavior. Increase by small increments the distance and direction changes until you can move around the kitchen while she stays. When working with the cat for duration and distraction, give her verbal feedback, telling her what a wonderful girl she is. Click and treat her when she does as requested.

Gradually add distractions and distance. Reinforce your cat when she stays.

With practice and patience, your cat will learn to politely sit and stay when doors are opened.

Gradually increase the distractions while training to stop door darting. While asking your cat to stay, turn the handle of the door. If she continues to stay, click and then give her a treat. If she tries to rush the door, ignore her by walking away, and give her a brief timeout. Try again a bit later, this time in an alternative location so she has a change in scenery. Using either the 300 Peck Pigeon technique or a variation, slowly increase the length of the *stay* while gradually adding distracting activities until you reach that ultimate distraction level—opening the door. If she sprints for the door, close it, give her a brief timeout, and then try again, setting the criteria lower. Be sure to occasionally change locations, working with your cat in other designated spots to strengthen the behavior in different circumstances and among a variety of distractions. Your cat should eventually sit and stay on request regardless of her location.

TREAT SPOTS FOR *STAY* BEHAVIORS

The door darter needs to be rewarded where she is being trained to stay. If you are teaching her to stay on a designated stool, then place the treat on the stool in front of her after the click. When helping her learn how to stay on request on her cat tree, treat her on the tree. Don't toss the treat off the stool or the tree, because you want her to learn to stay for increasing lengths of time in one spot on request.

Case Study: Door Darting

SITUATION: Leo is a large, gorgeous spotted male who is adored and admired by all who meet him. Linda bought him from a breeder when he was five months old. Leo is a very affectionate and active cat, and he loves to be with Linda, following her around the apartment from room to room.

When Linda purchased Leo, the breeder told her that Leo could be walked on a leash. Linda thought it would be fun to show him off to the neighborhood and was looking forward to walking him to her best friend's house on the next block. She purchased a walking jacket and a leash and followed the breeder's instructions for acclimating Leo to them. After about two weeks of practice, Linda felt that she and Leo were ready to venture out into the world.

The day finally came for Leo's debut. The walk was fun, he met the neighbors, and everyone admired and stroked him. Leo loved the attention and looked regal as he walked. At first, Linda thought the outing was a success. Her initial assessment changed, though, the day after the walk, when Leo started running to the front door and meowing whenever Linda opened it. The behavior escalated. Within a week, Leo was howling at the doors and windows and attempting to race out at every potential opportunity. Leo did manage to escape a couple of times, but luckily Linda was able to coax him back in with his favorite chicken treat. Linda called me two months after the original door-darting incident, asking for help.

ASSESSMENT: Leo's walk caused him to want more. Outside was so much more fascinating than inside, and everyone he met showered him with attention. What more could a handsome fellow ask for?

During my initial visit to Linda and Leo, I noticed that the well-decorated apartment was boring from a cat's viewpoint. Linda didn't own any cat furniture or window perches for Leo to climb on, and there were no challenging cat toys for him. In addition, Linda's work schedule was intense, so she wasn't able to spend as much time with Leo as she would have liked.

RECOMMENDATIONS: I recommended that Linda clicker-train Leo and convert her apartment into a more fun and cat-centric space. Leo and Linda also needed to implement a consistent play, feeding, quality-time, and clicker-training schedule.

Linda added two tall cat trees, one in the bedroom and one in the living room. She placed the cat tree in the living room on the opposite side of the room from the front door. Both trees had wide shelves, perfect for Leo to lounge on. We designated one of the shelves on the living-room tree as one of "Leo's spots;" the other spot was a stool in the kitchen. Leo was also presented with new interactive toys and food puzzles. Because play is important, Linda started using a fishing-pole toy, playing in a way that imitated hunting.

Linda started to clicker-train Leo immediately. He caught on quickly, eager for the challenge. By the second session, he was sitting on both of his designated spots when requested. Linda then taught him to stay on the cat tree, lengthening the time gradually. She added the verbal cue *stay* after Leo had learned to stay for five seconds. At seven seconds, Leo hit a plateau, jumping off of the cat tree and rushing to rub Linda's legs. Linda reset the behavior and used a variation of the 300 Peck Pigeon technique, clicking and treating him at four seconds, then working up to five seconds. Every time Linda reached the infamous seven-second mark, Leo would behave the same way, jumping off the tree and rubbing Linda's legs. As far as Linda knew, she wasn't doing anything to reinforce this.

Linda videotaped the event for me. I noticed that every time Leo rubbed Linda's legs, she unconsciously reached down and gave his tail a loving tweak. Both Leo and Linda were reinforcing the behavior, Leo by rubbing Linda's legs and Linda by giving him attention as she affectionately tweaked his tail.

I advised Linda to start over, this time working with Leo on the stool in the kitchen. I also asked her to position herself in back of the counter instead of right next to the stool. Linda started over at the *one Savannah* count, encouraging Leo by saying "good boy, Leo," and was able to work him into a ten-second *stay* very quickly.

Once the plateau was breached, Linda gradually added distractions and movement. She started by stepping back and then around Leo. Linda increased her distance and movements by small increments each time. When Leo reached other plateaus, Linda would switch locations and restart the count, reinforcing a few seconds in at a low distraction level and then gradually building both distractions and duration.

Doors were the next challenge. Leo was now able to stay on the stool for fifteen seconds despite distractions and movement. Linda asked for a *stay* and walked up to the door. Leo sat still, watching her every move intensely. Linda clicked and walked back to him, giving him his favorite treat. She then pushed it a little more, walking up to the door and touching the handle. Leo still stayed, so Linda clicked and treated him. This time she walked up to the door, turned the handle, and opened the door a quarter of an inch. Leo was off his chair in a flash and at the door. Linda closed the door as he was running toward it, turned away from Leo, walked out of the room, and closed a door between them.

After an appropriate timeout of about two minutes, Linda patiently cued Leo back to his spot on the cat tree. Using a variation of the 300 Peck Pigeon, she asked Leo to stay for a minute and thirty seconds, a duration of time for which he was adept at staying, and then gradually increased both the distractions and the duration of the stay. It took multiple sessions, but Leo finally stopped seeing doors as invitations to the Indy 500.

The Art of Scratching

Scratching objects is normal behavior for cats. The act of scratching is important for both the psychological and physical health of the cat. Along with nail maintenance, cats scratch to mark territory, to relieve stress, and to be playful. Additionally, when cats scratch, they provide themselves with a good stretch. Unfortunately, the objects on which they sometimes choose to exercise their claws drive their favorite people into frustration and despair.

Cats do have to scratch, but they don't have to scratch your brand-new sofa or rug.

Sometimes people think that declawing is the answer to the furniture-scratching challenge. Instead of declawing, consider training your cat and providing him with appropriate cat-centric furniture to scratch.

THE SCRATCHING SOLUTIONS TOOL KIT

- Primary reinforcer (treats)
- Secondary reinforcer (clicker)
- Deterrent (wide double-sided tape)
- Alternative scratching surfaces (horizontal and vertical scratchers)

Training is easier, less expensive, pain free, and fun while building the bond between the cat and her people. Again, cats are smart, and they learn very quickly. Clicker training, when combined with management, is very effective at stopping cats from slicing and dicing the furniture.

Sherlock Toes

Scratching objects satisfies a variety of the cat's fundamental needs. Besides the obvious nail maintenance, a few of the other reasons cats scratch include: communicating, stretching, fulfilling emotional needs, and attracting attention. Let's put our detective hats on again and figure out what motivates your cat. Once you know the primary reasons that cats scratch, you can modify the behavior through a few changes to the environment and, of course, clicker training.

Manicures

Scratching is nature's way of giving cats the perfect manicure. While we humans spend lots of hours and money on prettying up our fingernails and toenails, all a cat has to do is find a scratchable object and scratch. Besides providing a good toe massage, scratching conditions the claws and removes old sheaths, allowing new, healthy ones to grow.

Here Ye, Hear Ye!

Because cats can't use cell phones to call their friends, nature has devised other effective communication systems for them. Scratching is one of these. In fact, scratching is probably one of the most effective communication tools that nature has invented. Scratching engages all of the senses at the same time. It broadcasts to the world through sight, sound, touch, and smell. I cannot think of any manmade communication system that can boast of that accomplishment.

Every cat has her own "claw print." The act of scratching creates visible grooves, announcing to the world who was there. Understandably, most people would rather have their cats announce their presence on something other than

> ## NO PUNISHMENT!
>
> Punishment doesn't work because:
> - It doesn't address the reasons the cat is scratching.
> - It doesn't provide a long-term solution; cats will continue to scratch when no one is looking.
> - It doesn't address the cat's natural instinct to scratch.
> - It can hurt a cat both physically and psychologically.
> - It can damage the bond between the cat and her person because cats associate the punishment with the punisher.

great-grandma's chair. Cats also broadcast information via scent glands located on the bottom of their paws. The scent is deposited on the scratched object. These scents are like press releases, communicating vital information about the scratcher to other cats.

Everyone recognizes the sound of a cat enjoying a good scratch. While we cringe when we hear the distinctive sound of the rug being shredded, the sound of scratching audibly announces the scratcher's presence and the extent of her territory to all cats within hearing distance.

Stretch

Nothing feels better than a good stretch. We can learn a lot from our furry little friends, including how to reach and stretch efficiently. Watch how a cat scratches a vertical object—she reaches as high as she can and scratches while simultaneously giving herself a healthy stretch. Typically, cats stretch and scratch after a satisfying nap. Horizontal scratchers also provide good opportunities for long, euphoric stretches while scratching.

All cats, including declawed cats, must scratch. Scratching satisfies many instinctual needs.

Cats sometimes stretch and scratch after they wake up from naps. Having designated places for them to do so is important.

Emotional Scratches

Sometimes cats scratch for emotional reasons. Often, cats in frisky moods will scratch their posts in anticipation of a good rollick or just to release playful energy. One of my cats scratches her favorite post when I come home after a day of consulting. She scratches and talks to me at the same time. Another one of my cats scratches in anticipation of a good meal and then again after an extended clicker-training session.

It is not unusual for cats to relieve tension and anxiety by dispersing energy through a scratching session. Ultimately, it is healthier for a cat to display her emotions by scratching a post than through unwanted stress-driven behaviors.

DECLAWED CATS NEED TO SCRATCH, TOO

Declawed cats need the same scratching opportunities as cats who have claws. They need to scratch for all of the same reasons that cats with claws scratch (with the exception of manicures).

Look at Me!

Some cats use their cat-smarts to manipulate their favorite humans for attention. These are the Attention Seekers. Remember them? You first met them in chapter 2 when they were jumping up on your counters. Scratching sofas, rugs, and chairs can be attention-seeking behavior that people inadvertently reinforce. Yelling, chasing the cat, and picking the cat up are examples of common responses that people have when confronted with their cats' bad scratching choices. These responses give the cat exactly what she wants—attention.

Cats will also scratch when playing and when they want to disperse energy.

Scratching the Right Stuff

The first step in training your cat to scratch the right stuff is to provide her with scratchers that she can really sink her claws into. Cats like choices, so your cat should have a variety of scratchers to choose from. Cats need both horizontal and vertical scratchers to satisfy all of their scratching urges. You should provide tall posts and horizontal and angled scratching surfaces in several different areas of the house. Because cats like to stretch, the vertical poles should ideally be high enough for your cat to have a full-length stretch with room to spare. The bases should be stable so that an exuberant cat doesn't pull the pole over on herself in the middle of an intense scratching session.

Provide your cat with both vertical posts and horizontal scratchers. Their textures should be different than those of your sofas and rugs.

Textures are important. If your cat is scratching the rug, don't provide her with a scratcher that is the same texture as the rug. Offering her a scratcher that feels the same as the forbidden surface will confuse her; she won't understand why the one surface is OK and the other is off limits. Instead, give her a scratching surface that feels different from the forbidden object. Most cats love the texture of sisal and corrugated cardboard. Tall poles wrapped in sisal rope and horizontal scratchers made from sisal-like materials or corrugated cardboard are available from a variety of sources.

Combination toys and scratchers are very popular for both cats and their favorite people. One of my favorites has a flat, round corrugated scratching area in the middle, surrounded by an open track that has a ping-pong ball in it. In addition to the ball, treats and toys can be placed in the track for fun. There is also a wedge-shaped scratcher available with a hole in each side that displays a dangling toy for the cat to bat around.

BUILD YOUR OWN SCRATCHING POST

Scratching posts can be expensive, but you can save money by building your own. A scratching post should be as tall as the cat is when he is stretched out, plus an additional 4 to 6 inches. The base of the scratching post needs to be solid and large so that the post can't be tipped over by an energetic cat. Sisal rope is a good choice for wrapping the post. Most cats love the feel of the sisal under their toes. The rope should neither be oiled nor treated with any chemicals.

The Alternative Experience

Now armed with the best scratchers and scratching posts for the job, you're ready to convince your cat that these objects are better to scratch than sofas and carpets. The basic strategy for accomplishing this is to make the previously scratched items unavailable for scratching while simultaneously providing more pleasing objects to scratch. It is very important to always give cats something better and more appealing than what has been taken from them.

Start modifying the cat's environment by making the forbidden areas unavailable. If it's a corner of a couch that your cat favors for scratching, cover it with wide double-sided tape, which doesn't feel good on a cat's toes. Cover the other corners of the couch with the tape, too, because your cat may decide, after finding that her favorite corner feels icky, to move operations to another corner.

Make sofas unpleasant places to scratch by covering them with placemats lined with double-sided sticky tape.

You can cover other areas with materials or fabrics that aren't fun or pleasant to scratch. For example, you can secure bed sheets, foil, or heavy plastic to the sofa. Placemats with double-sided tape on one side are also helpful for keeping cats from scratching the furniture. Use your imagination. Whatever non-cat-centric materials you use, make sure that they are taped down or tucked in so that your cat can't remove them or scratch underneath them.

Once the areas are covered, you need to give the cat an alternative and better object to scratch. If your cat is favoring an arm of the sofa, place one of the tall scratching posts directly in front of the now-covered-up arm. It won't work if you put the scratching post across the room, miles away from the scratched area of the sofa. Expect your living room to be a monument to your cat and his creativity for a little while, with scratching posts in front of sofas and everything covered in sheets and double-sided tape.

If your cat prefers to scratch the Oriental rug, either put deterrents (such as cheap placemats covered in double-sided tape) on the rug or put a sisal scratching mat on top of or adjacent to the scratched surface. You may have to temporarily hopscotch over the placemats or scratchers, or navigate around them. You can also use large objects such as cat-safe potted plants to block the scratched areas. To give your cat a pleasing alternative to the now-off-limits spot, place a horizontal scratcher next to the area.

When making the sofa unavailable for scratching, provide appropriate furniture and scratchers that are more fun to scratch.

Cats sometimes have tactical reasons for choosing areas to scratch. Prime scratching locations include those that are perfectly situated for territorial markers. Sometimes these areas are corners of the sofas nearest to where a cat's favorite person likes to sit. Scratching them will broadcast ownership rights to the world. Other times, locations are chosen because the fabric texture feels good, the furniture is at an ideal height, or the rug is perfectly situated for stretching and scratching. No matter the reason for the cat's preferred scratching locations, place scratching posts and horizontal scratchers directly on top or next to them. Putting acceptable scratching areas directly on top or in front of the target areas will both block the target areas and simultaneously allow the cat to express her property rights.

Reinforce

The stage is set. The rug and the antique sofa are now unavailable to sharp little claws. Horizontal and vertical scratchers that satisfy even the most finicky cat's scratching urges have been placed next to or on top of the covered areas. It's now time to roll up your sleeves, get the clicker out, and start reinforcing your cat's good behavior. The clicker is a very important communication tool and will reinforce the concept that the scratchers are good places to scratch.

Reinforce your cat when she scratches the scratching posts and horizontal scratchers by clicking once and then treating her.

REPLACEMENT THERAPY RULE

Don't forget the replacement therapy rule! Whenever you make an area unavailable for scratching, you must provide your cat with something that is better and more fun to scratch. It should feel good under her toes, certainly better than that silly old sofa, which now feels all weird and sticky.

The very first exercise of pairing the clicker with something motivating, detailed in chapter 1, is vital for reinforcing proper scratching behavior. After your cat has a strong clicker foundation, associating the sound of the clicker with something enjoyable, you are ready to reinforce good scratching habits.

Every time you see your kitty scratching the surface you want her to scratch, click and then give her a treat. As usual, timing is crucial. Her behavior needs to be reinforced with a click while she's in the process of scratching the right surface. Clicking her before or after she scratches the right area isn't very effective because the click reinforces the behavior that is being performed at the instant of the click.

In addition to working toward perfectly timed clicks, watch for wasted clicks. In other words, make each click count. Click only when the cat is performing the correct behavior. If you click without reason, the clicker will lose its power.

If your cat has a strong clicker foundation and your motivator is truly motivating, it won't take long to convince her to use the appropriate scratchers and to ignore the forbidden areas. If she does slip up and scratch an undesirable object, don't click and treat. Instead, make the area off limits to her and provide her with another acceptable surface to scratch.

It can be challenging to invite guests in and ask them to sit and make themselves at home on sofas and chairs that are both covered with sticky tape and crowded with posts and scratchers. But with patience and effective clicker work, your furniture will become tape free again in no time. Once your cat is consistently scratching the cat-centric furniture, gradually move the posts and scratchers to a more convenient area. Move them an inch every day until you reach your goal. The posts and scratchers do need to be in the same room as the sofa that was being scratched, but they don't have to be located right next to the targeted sofa once your cat is in the habit of scratching the appropriate cat-centric furniture.

Don't forget to click and treat your cat when you see her scratching the posts and horizontal scratchers. If you find that your cat starts scratching the wrong areas again, you are probably getting a little impatient and moving the posts too quickly. Put them back and proceed a little slower.

After your cat is consistently scratching the posts and scratchers in their final locations, you can gradually remove the double-sided tape, one piece at a time. Take your time for the sake of your furniture; you want to ensure that your cat is consistently scratching the posts and horizontal scratchers before removing the next strip of tape. It may take a week or longer to remove it all.

Cats use scratching posts and horizontal scratchers to mark their territory by both scratching and rubbing.

The Zen of Clipping Nails

Keeping your cat's nails trimmed will help maintain the health of her nails and reduce collateral damage. Many strong people who consider themselves fearless in life cower at the thought of trimming their cat's nails. They arm themselves with towels, bandages, gloves, and an extra pair of hands. They also prepare themselves for what they consider the inevitable: a traumatized cat who won't come near them for days.

Clicker training is a very effective way of making clipping your cat's nails a stress-free experience.

Clipping nails doesn't have to be a near-death experience. Clicker training can be used to desensitize cats to nail clipping. Start by lightly touching your cat's toes with your fingers. If she doesn't show any nervousness or anxiety, click and treat her. The treat needs to be one of her favorites, with a high motivation factor, because you are asking her to participate in an activity that most cats highly dislike. If she leaves or doesn't

ASIA'S ESSENTIAL TOE MASSAGE

Asia, a Bengal cat with whom I share my life, is different than most cats. Not only does he enjoy having his back claws clipped but he also loves getting evening toe massages. It wasn't always like that, though. When he first came to live with me, he did not want anyone messing with his feet. Because he had been declawed in the front by his former person, he had extreme toe sensitivity, making it next to impossible to touch or trim his back claws.

Asia adores dehydrated organic chicken and enjoys the challenge of clicker training. Every night, starting at 8:00 p.m., Asia has clicker-training sessions. Initially, two sessions every night focused on toe desensitization. After about two weeks of work and lots of clicks and dehydrated chicken, Asia finally allowed me to massage his back feet and toes. At first, the massages were short and light; they then gradually lengthened. Now, Asia waits patiently for his toe massages every evening, rolling onto his back, extending a back foot, and spreading his toes.

want her toes touched, don't click and treat. Also, don't insist. Wait and try again at a later time when she's more relaxed. A good time to approach your kitty is when she's content and lying down.

Persevere and be patient. Because your cat understands the concepts of clicker training, she'll quickly understand that if she lets you touch her toes, she'll get a click and a yummy treat. After your cat lets you touch her toes, gradually increase the time for which you touch each of them. Once she allows the extended touch to each toe, add a little gentle pressure. Click and treat her only when she is relaxed and accepting of the increased toe touching and pressure. At the smallest sign of displeasure, stop and do not click and treat. Wait a few hours or try again the next day, starting over from scratch and proceeding slower.

Keep desensitizing and working with your cat until you can give her light toe massages. Don't forget to click and treat, reinforcing the toe-massage experience. Eventually, each little toe can be massaged and lightly pressed to extend the nail. Soon, terror-free nail clipping can commence.

It's important to stop at the first signs of stress or displeasure when desensitizing your cat to nail clipping. Try again later, proceeding slower.

Before clipping your cat's nails, introduce her to the nail clipper by letting her sniff it. If she doesn't display anxiety, click and treat her as she sniffs. Next, touch her lightly with the nail clipper on different parts of her body, clicking and treating her when she shows no nervousness or displeasure. Finally, touch the top of her toes on one paw with the clipper, and click and treat her if she's accepting of the experience. If the clipper upsets her, then stop the session and continue later, starting over and proceeding at a slower, lighter pace. It's best to have many short sessions spread out over a few days than to have long sessions.

After your cat allows gentle handling of her toes and is nonchalant about the nail clipper, press one toe to extend the nail. If your cat is fine with the experience, cut the tip of the nail. Be careful that you don't clip too close to the quick (the pinkish area in the nail that contains a blood vessel and a nerve); it can be painful and bleed if cut. Go slow; don't expect to do all the nails in one sitting. In the beginning, it may take a couple of days to clip all of her nails.

Case Study: Furniture Scratching

SITUATION: Mr. Moon is an artist's cat. Appropriately, Mr. Moon is a work of art himself—a white cat with delicate black paintbrush markings on his forehead. As lovely as Mr. Moon is, he upsets Ellen, his mom, on a daily basis by scratching the rugs. He has both vertical and horizontal scratchers available to him, but he prefers the rugs. Ellen noticed that he prefers certain rug textures, which just happen to make up the majority of the rugs in the house. Mr. Moon is also partial to scratching certain areas, mostly those areas in front of closed doors to the rooms where Ellen periodically works. Sometimes he follows Ellen around the house, pausing from time to time to scratch. Not coincidentally, his inappropriate scratching only occurs when Ellen is home. Her husband has observed that Mr. Moon is always perfectly behaved when the other members of the household are present. Mr. Moon only engages in this annoying and destructive behavior around Ellen.

Ellen adores Mr. Moon and has tried everything she can think of to stop the behavior. She's picked him up, petted him, played with him, and, in frustration, yelled at him. One time, she tried squirting him with a squirt bottle, but he slinked away and didn't come near her for hours. She felt awful.

ASSESSMENT: Mr. Moon is an Attention Seeker, using scratching as a way to elicit attention from Ellen. In her attempts to stop the behavior, Ellen has inadvertently reinforced the behavior by interacting with him in various ways. Mr. Moon has a very strong bond with Ellen, and will do just about anything for attention from her.

RECOMMENDATIONS:

I recommended a combination of management and clicker training. Ellen threw away the squirt bottle and made the rugs uncomfortable places to scratch by putting placemats covered with double-sided tape on the scratched areas. Because Mr. Moon likes sisal textures, Ellen placed horizontal scratchers and vertical scratching posts covered with sisal next to the areas made inaccessible by the tape.

Before using the clicker for reinforcing proper scratching behavior, Ellen worked with Mr. Moon so that he associated the sound of the clicker with his favorite treat. Once Mr. Moon understood the significance of the click, Ellen began positively reinforcing Mr. Moon for scratching the correct surfaces. Every time Mr. Moon scratched either the horizontal scratchers or vertical posts, she clicked and then tossed him a treat. Ellen also made sure to not interact with him, turning her back to him and leaving the room, when he found other, inappropriate places to scratch. It took patience and consistency, but Mr. Moon finally understood that he only got attention from Ellen when he scratched the correct surfaces. He also enjoyed the quality time he now had with Ellen. The clicker training was so much fun and so successful that Ellen proceeded to teach Mr. Moon some new behaviors, such as going to his special mat, sitting, shaking hands, and giving her kisses on cue. Mr. Moon learned that he did not need to scratch in order to have Ellen's full and undivided attention. Through clicker training, blocking areas from sharp nails, and adding appropriate scratching surfaces, Ellen was able to reinforce the correct behavior and give Mr. Moon the attention he craved.

CHAPTER 5

Matchmaking Skills

You might be convinced that the adorable puff of fur you just adopted is the perfect buddy for your cat, but don't be surprised if your cat has a different viewpoint. Instead of seeing the newcomer as adorable and welcoming her with open paws, your resident cat will probably see her as an invader.

Cats are individuals, each with their own preferences and personalities. Choosing a cat you think is a perfect match for your resident cat isn't that simple. Just because you think the cats should be friends doesn't guarantee that they will be. You can greatly increase the odds that they will be able to live peacefully together by gradually introducing them to each other in a way that encourages amicable feelings between them.

INTRODUCTION TOOL KIT

- **Primary reinforcer** (treats)
- **Secondary reinforcer** (clicker)
- **Means of pheromone exchange** (socks and towels)
- **Means of interaction** (food and double-ended toys)

The Secret

The secret to a stress-free introduction is encouraging fun, shared experiences between the cats while they are confined away from each other. At first glance, this sounds a little awkward, and slightly impossible. Not true! Cats can build friendly relationships without meeting nose-to-nose by participating in a series of activities.

Successful introductions can take a few weeks, a few months, or sometimes longer. Clicker training used in conjunction with introduction techniques can make the difference between a smooth transition and a blitzkrieg.

School Is in Session

Think of the introduction process as sending your cats to school to earn a degree in Social Interactions. Unlike public school, cat etiquette school doesn't follow a schedule. It's an experimental, self-paced school that operates in cat time. Cats move on to the next grade only after they have successfully completed the exercises set forth in the previous grade level.

CHOOSING A BUDDY

There's never a guarantee that cats will become best friends. You can increase the odds of a friendship by carefully choosing a new cat based on the history, age, and personalities of both cats. Here are a few guidelines:

- Match cats up who have the same activity and energy level.
- Adopt a cat who has a history of getting along well with other cats.
- Try to match ages. If you have a senior cat who enjoys napping, don't adopt a kitten.
- If you know your cat does not get along with other cats, don't adopt another cat.

First Grade

- Pheromone exchanges: pet each cat with a clean sock or soft towel. Exchange, placing the sock or towel used on one cat where the other cat walks.
- Clicker training: the secondary reinforcer needs to have first been paired with a motivator such as food. Click and treat only when the cats are around the socks without displaying anxiety or aggression.

Second Grade

- Pheromone exchanges: gradually inch the scented socks toward the cats' sleeping areas. Continue to click and treat for positives around the socks.
- Breaking bread: feed cats simultaneously on either side of a closed door. Start by putting the food dishes 4 to 6 feet from the door. Gradually inch feeding stations toward the door at each meal.

Third Grade

- Pheromone exchanges: continue to exchange pheromones, clicking and treating as before; treats should be placed on the socks.
- Breaking bread: continue feeding cats on both sides of the closed door.
- Shared play: encourage the cats to play with each other under the door using a double-ended toy.

Fourth Grade

- Pheromone exchanges: continue the scent exchange.
- Breaking bread: feed the cats with the door open. Feeding stations should be backed away from the door; the one in the new cat's room should be deep inside the room, and the other one should be at least one room's length away. Close the door after the food has been eaten. After each meal, increase the time that the door is left open by one second. Close the door at the first sign of aggression or stress.

Fifth Grade

- Peaceful coexistence: allow supervised visits and gradually extend the amount of time they're allowed to spend together. When the cats are peacefully together in the same room, mark the event with a click and treats, being sure to treat the cat who is the most food-motivated first.
- Clicker training: continue to train both cats. By this point, you can start training them together. Each cat should have her own stool or mat and sit on cue.

the curriculum

Student Orientation: Laying the Foundation

Do everything you can to make the transition as easy as possible for the cats and for your family. Before the new cat comes home, have a special room set up just for her. She will need food, water, a litter box, a comfortable bed, and places to climb. Her room should be as comfortable and full of enrichment as possible. This room will be her safety zone, a quiet area that is off limits to all other animals.

If possible, do a little homework about your new cat's history. Find out what food she enjoys as well as what her favorite treats are. Inquire about the type of cat litter and box she used in her previous home. Maybe her litter box can come with her. If she's a mystery cat with no recorded history, provide her with an appropriately sized litter box that is uncovered and has never been used by another cat. Cats like consistency and familiarity. If you are lucky and have access to the litter box she used in her previous situation, scoop about one cup of litter from it and put it in a plastic bag. After putting about 2 to 3 inches of fresh litter in the new box, add the litter secured from her original box so that the box smells familiar to her.

Cats need consistency. If possible, provide your new cat with the same brand of litter she's used to using.

MEDICAL CHECKUP

Make sure that your new cat has a complete medical checkup and that she is current on her vaccinations, has been wormed, and is disease-free before you bring her into your home to meet your resident cat. If she is sick, isolate her completely from other animals.

If possible, bring her belongings with her from her previous home. Favorite toys will help the newbie adjust to her new digs. If the newcomer was attached to her previous person, ask the person to sleep in an old T-shirt and then place the shirt in the carrier to help her feel a little more secure.

Cats who feel frightened and insecure will appreciate hiding places such as boxes or paper bags with the handles removed that are laid on their sides. This room will be your new cat's sanctuary while you introduce her to your resident cat. Having her own room will help her feel safe and confident, making the introductions less stressful for her.

Getting to Know Your New Friend

Every cat is unique. Some cats immediately adjust to their new homes; others need time to feel secure and confident. It is normal for a shy cat to retreat under the bed or sofa, preferring to assess her new world from a safe location. A cat with more confidence might explore her new surroundings. Whether your cat is shy or brave, don't force her to say hello to you by picking her up or by grabbing her. Let her initiate the first greeting.

Cats like formality and respect. Greet a cat by extending your index finger toward the cat at the cat's nose level. Your finger can be anywhere from 6 inches to several feet away. If the cat wants to say hello, she'll come up to your finger, first touching it with her nose and then turning her head so that your finger is on the side of her mouth. She will continue to move her head until your finger is on her cheek, where she can rub it. By doing this, she is marking you with her greeting pheromones. After the initial greeting, she will most likely appreciate you gently stroking her under her chin, on her neck, and on the back of her head. After

Each cat is an individual. Some cats adjust quickly to a new home; others hide, taking longer to adjust.

EQUAL TIME FOR THE FIRST CAT

Your resident cat needs equal attention so that she doesn't feel like the third wheel. Make sure to spend quality time with her, playing and giving her lots of love. Clicker training will strengthen your relationship, helping to reassure her that she's still your best girl. Clicking will also provide the preliminary groundwork for the coming introductions.

Cats have scent glands located on their cheeks that produce friendly or greeting pheromones.

the cat is comfortable with her neck and head area being stroked, you can stroke and pet her back and sides.

Build a friendly relationship with your new cat before introducing her to the resident cat. It might be love at first sight, or it may take a while for her to warm up to you. You can heavily sway her opinion of you with food that she can't resist. Every time you visit her, arm yourself with tiny pieces of tasty treats. Clicker training will also help you earn your new cat's trust and build bonds between you.

The First Clicks

Start clicker training immediately after the newcomer has settled into her new room. If she is shy, consider using as the secondary reinforcer a ballpoint pen or another device that makes a subtle, soft sound. The sound of the clicker may be too loud for your little newcomer. Wrapping the clicker in a sock will also soften the sound, making it easier on a cat's ears. A braver, more secure cat should have no problem with the standard i-Click clicker. The simple act of pairing the clicker with something positive, as covered in chapter 1, will help you build your relationship with your new cat and will later encourage camaraderie between her and your resident cat.

TRAINING MULTIPLE CATS

Having more than one cat doesn't mean that you have to search high and low for multiple reinforcer devices that make unique sounds. You can use the same device for all of your cats. When working with multiple cats, direct your attention and the clicker toward the cat from whom you are requesting a behavior. The cats will understand.

You also have the option of buying a clicker that has multiple tones. I prefer using one clicker because, in the heat of the clicker moment, I find it is less confusing to use one device.

First Grade

Your cats are ready to start first grade when the newbie has bonded to you, has adjusted to her new room, and is enjoying her regular meals and treats. Additionally, both cats need to be well versed in the basics of clicker training.

The first grade will concentrate on social-skill building through scent exchanges. Cats produce pheromones, some of which are friendlier than others. When a cat greets you, she will rub you with her cheek and her head, marking you with her scent. These scents are produced by sebaceous glands and are considered the friendly pheromones; they are the cat version of "hello, it's nice to meet you."

We will take advantage of these built-in welcome-wagon pheromones and introduce the cats to each other remotely through pheromone exchanges. Before starting the scent exchange, you'll need to make sure that you have several pairs of socks and a few small, soft towels on hand. They do not have to be designer socks—any style or color will do—they just have to be clean and soft. Used socks and towels are fine, too, as long as they are clean.

Begin the exchange by gently petting your resident cat's cheek, stroking her gently in one direction, toward her ear, with one of the clean socks. Pet the newcomer's cheek with another clean sock.

Introduce the cats through scent exchanges. First, gently pet each cat's cheek with a separate new or laundered sock.

After you've gathered the pheromones from both cats, place the resident cat's sock in the newbie's room. Be careful not to put the sock where she eats or sleeps, or near her litter box. Next, take the sock with the newcomer's scent on it and place it in an area where your resident cat likes to hang out—again, not near her food, sleeping quarters, or litter box. If your schedule allows, exchange scents twice a day—once in the morning and once in the evening—using clean socks each time. Leave the socks out for the cats in between exchanges.

Pheromone exchanges are similar to phone calls—the cats will be sizing each other up and getting to know each other without meeting nose-to-nose.

Clicking and treating each time your cats respond favorably to the other's scent-laden sock will help establish a friendly relationship.

Because every cat is different and every introduction is unique, it is hard to say how many days the initial pheromone exchange will take. Some cats accept each other's scent after a few days while others can take a week or longer.

If you've done your homework, both cats are by this stage strongly schooled in the basics of clicker training and are eager to work. The combination of the clicker training and the scent exchanges will send a double amicable message to both cats, helping to establish a friendly relationship between the two strangers while they are still separated from each other.

Every time either cat sniffs the sock with the other's scent on it, show your approval by immediately clicking and then tossing her a treat. The timing has to be spot-on perfect. The click needs to be simultaneous with the cat pleasantly interacting with the sock. Neutral responses are the same as positive responses. Click and then treat whenever either cat walks nonchalantly by the sock. Some cats become excited by the scent-laced socks and carry them around, roll on them, or sleep on them. Reward this behavior, as well, with a click and a treat. Clicking and treating the positive interactions with the scent-laden socks helps to encourage, build, and reinforce a positive relationship between the cats.

When either cat is displaying any signs of nervousness, aggression, or discomfort around the socks, do not click. Clicking while a cat is unhappy or upset will reinforce those emotions. Learn to

A DIFFERENT APPROACH

If your cat is doing everything she can to avoid the scent-laden sock when you first put it down, consider a remedial education class. Place the sock somewhere that is inaccessible to your cat for a few hours so the pheromones lose their intensity. After the pheromones dissipate, place the sock back in her space. She should accept the sock when the scent loses its concentration.

watch for both subtle and not-so-subtle body language, and when you see signs of aggression, stress, or nervousness, ignore them.

It's OK if your cat responds to the socks with hisses, avoidance, or negative emotions. Look at it as an important learning tool. The cats' responses to the socks will give you an idea of how long your cats will be in school. Don't reprimand, punish, or yell at them if they are taking a little longer to acclimate to the scents.

Your cats are ready to move on to the next grade when they are both comfortable with each other's scented socks. This may take a few days, a week, or longer. The cats will tell you when they are ready through their body language and actions, either displaying friendly interest in the socks or acting neutral around them. Moving on to the next grade level should be based on the response from the cat who is having the most problems with accepting the pheromone-laced socks. You can proceed only as fast as the cat with the most challenges will allow. Celebrate your cat's advancement to second grade with treats and affection. While you're at it, pat yourself on the back and celebrate your success with a click and the kind of treat that motivates *you*.

In preparation for future lessons, continue to increase each cat's clicker training skills until they both easily follow the target, stand on their own placemats, and sit on cue. Working with both cats will also help increase their sense of security and strengthen and build the relationships you have with both cats.

FIELD TRIPS

Help your new cat become familiarized with the sights, smells, and sounds of her new home by letting her check out the rest of the house. The cats will need to remain separated from each other during the exploration. After the field trips, return the newcomer to her own room.

It may take a few days, a week, or longer until your cats are each responding favorably to the other's pheromone-laced sock.

Second Grade

Now that your cats are in the second grade, it's time to add another activity to their training. This one revolves around everyone's favorite pastime—eating. The goal is for the cats to break bread together while still separated by the closed door. You will need delicious food that the cats adore. Start by placing the feeding stations about 4 to 6 feet away from each side of the closed door. If your cats refuse to eat because they are stressed over their close proximity to each other, back the stations further away from the door until they are at a comfortable eating distance. Decrease the distance from the door by 1 to 2 inches per feeding until the feeding stations are close to each other, still on opposite sides of the closed door. You will know if you are expecting too much too fast if the cats refuse to eat or exhibit aggressive behaviors. If your match-making tactics prove to be too optimistic, move the dishes back to a comfortable distance and proceed more slowly.

Continue the pheromone exchanges twice a day, using clean socks each time, but with a change in venue. The sock location should change gradually—the goal being each cat's favorite napping area. At each scent exchange, slowly inch the socks toward each cat's individual sleeping area. Take your time, moving the socks about an inch at a time, over a period of days. Move them only when the cats are responding positively or neutrally around the socks, displaying no signs of unhappiness, aggression, or stress. If you hurry the process and place the pheromone-scented sock directly in your cat's sleeping quarters, she will probably abandon the spot and seek out a safer, scent-free place to nap.

Don't forget the clicker during this process. Clicker training will help fight the boredom blues and will stimulate the cats. Keep clicking and then treating for positive and neutral responses to the socks. You can keep things interesting for both you and the cats by continuing clicker training in other respects. After they stand when requested on their mats, teach them to sit, stay, and shake.

Your little Einsteins are ready for the third grade after they are sleeping on the other's scented sock and are eating comfortably next to each other while separated by the closed door.

Before each meal, both cats' feeding stations should be moved 1–2 inches toward the closed door that keeps them separated.

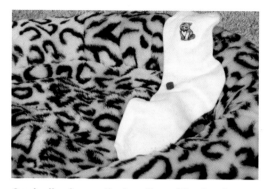
Gradually change the location of the treats until the cats are comfortable with eating them directly off of the pheromone-scented socks.

Third Grade

Your cats will need to keep practicing the social skills they learned in the first and second grades by continuing to eat near each other and by exchanging pheromones. There will be one change to the pheromone exercise, though. Continue the pheromone exchange as before, except change the treat location. After clicking, put the treats directly on the socks. If your cat refuses to eat the treat, place it near the sock and gradually move it with each click/treat cycle closer to and, finally, on top of the sock.

The next activity on the curriculum involves play. The goal is for the cats to play with each other under the door with the aid of a double-ended toy. The toy you use can make a big difference and can help influence the cats to take life less seriously. Whatever toy you choose, it should be a toy with an irresistible something on each end. The toy needs to be able to easily slip under the door so that both cats can play with it simultaneously while still separated by the closed door. If your schedule allows it, encourage play a few times a day.

Encouraging the cats to play with each other under the door will only work if both cats enjoy playing. Otherwise, you may find that one cat is having a blast while the other looks for something more interesting to do. You can't force them to have a good time. If one or both of your cats don't enjoy playing, then don't insist on it. Instead, spend more time on group activities that everyone can enjoy, such as eating together on opposite sides of the closed door.

Your cats are ready to move on to the fourth grade after they are eating treats off of each other's scented socks, and they play nicely and eat together while separated by the closed door.

Encouraging your cats to play with each other under the door will help them develop a friendly relationship with each other.

Fourth Grade

Wow—your cats are now in the fourth grade! They deserve a special treat for their continuing success.

It goes without saying that you will continue the closed-door play dates and the pheromone exchanges as described in the third grade.

Food continues to be vital for encouraging the cats to accept each other. The food for this next exercise needs to be adored and coveted by both cats—something so savory and tasty that no other cat or activity could distract them from the fine-dining experience.

Spend quality time with each cat every day. Scheduling activities the cats can enjoy individually will help them feel more secure.

Start by backing the feeding stations away from the door. Move the newbie's feeding station deep into her sanctuary room; the other one should be placed down the hall or, if possible, one room's length away from the sanctuary room. They need to be placed so that the cats can hear and smell, and maybe see, each other enjoying their feasts when you finally open the door to the confinement room.

Take a deep breath and live dangerously. Put the bowls of delicious food down for each cat and then open the door that separates them so that both cats are eating simultaneously. They won't be near each other, but they will be able to hear and possibly see each other enjoying their meals. As soon as the first cat finishes her meal, close the door to the room. Every meal should be fed in this fashion. Extend the time that you leave the door open after each meal by one second only if there are no indications of problems.

Watch the cats' body language. At the first sign of any potential aggression, such as fixated eyes, constricted pupils, stalking, unfriendly vocalizations, thumping tails, or flattened ears or whiskers,

SAFETY FIRST

It is very important to always supervise cats when they are playing with toys that have strings, wires, or other potentially dangerous pieces. In between play times, place these toys somewhere where the cats can't access them. Safety comes first, and accidents can happen, such as a cat's becoming entangled in strings or swallowing toy parts, so make sure that these types of toys are not available for the cats to play with when you are not around to supervise.

close the door. At the next meal, don't leave the door open as long and proceed more slowly, gradually adding time at a slower pace. Remember, you are operating in cat time. Sometimes it takes longer for cats to start accepting each other.

Move the feeding stations at least 10 feet away from the door and open the door while the cats eat. Close the door at the first signs of aggression or stress.

You and your cats are ready to move on to the next grade when the cats have been peacefully eating together for several days without the benefit of the closed door. Additionally, they should still be enjoying their play dates and continue to respond well to the sock exchanges.

Fifth Grade

Gradually extend the cats' times together. These visits must be supervised. At the first sign of anxiety or aggression, separate the cats and take it slower. The hardest part of this long introduction process is our own impatience. We want the cats to get along, we would love for them to snuggle and play together, and we would like these things to happen ASAP.

Clicker training is very helpful during these social meetings. When the cats are in the same room together without anxiety or aggression, click once and treat both of them. (Treat the cat who is the biggest Foodie first.) Click and treat them when they peacefully coexist on the same pieces of furniture, such as sofas or cat trees.

In time your cats may become best buddies, eventually eating and cuddling together.

When clicker training cats together, work only on behaviors that both cats know. If you try to teach one cat a new trick the other already knows, they may both become distracted.

Both cats can be clicker-trained simultaneously at this point. Each cat should have her own stool or another prop to stand on. Start by having both cats stand and then sit on their stools or props, and work through only the behaviors that they already know. When teaching new behaviors, it's important to separate the cats; otherwise, they will distract each other. After they learn new behaviors, such as shaking hands, giving high fives, and staying, separately, work with them together, each on her own stool. Continue to expand their repertoire. Cats who click together stay together.

ASSIGNMENT FOR THE TEACHER

Cats are very good communicators. Pay attention and read the communication signals that they are broadcasting. The cats will let you know through vocalizations and body language if you are trying to force the friendship too quickly. An unhappy or upset cat may growl, scream, or hiss; her ears or whiskers may flatten against her head; and her tail may thump or move rapidly. Unhappy cats sometimes make themselves scarce, hiding from everyone. Other indications of introductions gone bad are the cat's pupils are either constricted or dilated and fixated on the other cat, and the body is in a stalking position. Sometimes an upset or anxious cat's skin will ripple. Chances are, if you see any of these signals while introducing cats to each other, you're pushing their relationship too fast and need to slow down.

Caviar and Sardines for All

Your cats are ready to graduate with honors from cat etiquette school and can share a dorm room when they can peacefully hang out together for extended lengths of time. They might not be best buddies, but they will need to tolerate each other and coexist without hostility or anxiety. Because every cat is an individual, it's difficult to predict how long it will be until they can stay together without supervision. Be patient. Some cats accept each other within weeks, while others take months. Don't rush the process; successful introductions take time and need to be done according to each cat's schedule.

HIGH PLACES

It is important that "vertical territory" with several levels is available for the cats to hang out on. Cats use vertical territory to peacefully work out their hierarchy. Where they position themselves in relation to each other and to you indicates their place in the hierarchy. Vertical territory should be located where the cats spend the most time. Tall cat trees, window perches, bookshelves, and secure wall shelves are a few examples of vertical territory. Be creative!

Because all cats are individuals and situations vary, it is hard to predict how long the introductions will take. To be successful, you must have patience.

Case Study:
Introductions

SITUATION: Ms. Daisy, a tiny two-and-a-half-year-old Russian Blue, had always ruled the Grahams' home. She always slept upstairs with Roberta, her favorite human, and spent her days either roaming the home or venturing outdoors. Sharing the house with Roberta and Ms. Daisy were Roberta's husband and two young children. After being pressured by the kids, Roberta decided to bring home a four-month-old female kitten named Iris from the shelter as a companion both for Daisy and for the children.

Roberta initially kept Iris in her own room, with the intention of gradually introducing the two cats to each other, but unfortunately there were a couple of unplanned and disastrous encounters early on. Roberta's husband accidentally opened the door to Iris's confinement room, resulting in her dashing out. Iris's intentions were obvious: she wanted to play with Daisy. But Daisy wanted nothing to do with her; instead, she hissed and ran away from the kitten. When Roberta contacted me, Daisy had started to spend most of her time walking around the house, hissing and growling. She refused to walk past the room where Iris was being confined.

ASSESSMENT: The cats were not properly introduced to each other.

RECOMMENDATIONS: Roberta immediately went to the closest discount store and bought dozens of little white socks. She also bought treats that both cats loved. Armed with socks, treats, and a couple of clickers, Roberta started pheromone exchanges and clicker training. Iris was particularly taken with Daisy's scent, rolling and burying herself in the socks. Daisy had the opposite reaction. Every time a freshly scented sock was put down next to her, she would hiss and growl at it, and then back away and stare at it. The good news was that Daisy immediately caught on to clicker training; within minutes, she was associating the clicker with a delicious treat and responding well to target training.

Once the degree of Daisy's agitation was established, we were able to develop an introduction plan. After Roberta gathered the kitten's pheromones, she placed the sock in a cabinet for a few hours so that the scent wasn't so intense. She then put the sock about 12 inches away from Daisy. Daisy went over to explore the sock. She sniffed it once without showing any signs of agitation. As she sniffed, Roberta clicked the clicker and then immediately tossed Daisy a treat.

Roberta counter-conditioned Daisy to the scented sock by gradually decreasing the time between gathering the kitten's pheromones and presenting the sock to

Daisy. Whenever Roberta saw Daisy go up to the sock or walk by the scented sock without any nervous or aggressive displays, she clicked and then treated Daisy. It took one week until Roberta was able to gather the pheromones and then immediately put the sock down next to Daisy without her getting agitated.

Our next goal was for Daisy to eat the treats off the socks. This took a week of gradually inching the treat closer to the sock until Daisy finally ate the treat directly off the sock.

Daisy enjoyed clicker training. Roberta had her target- and mat-trained by the time she was eagerly eating treats off the socks with the kitten's scent on them. She was also especially fond of following the target around the house.

Roberta took advantage of Daisy's love of treats and target training by gradually leading her with the target close to Iris's room. Whenever Roberta treated Daisy, she would toss the treat a little closer to the door. After a couple of weeks of work, Daisy finally walked by the door and started to show mild interest in the little paw that extended under it.

After they'd cleared the first hurdle, and Daisy started showing interest in Iris as a possible play buddy, Roberta started feeding both cats at the same time, separated by the closed door. Roberta first placed the feeding stations far apart from each other, and gradually reduced the distance to the closed door by 1 inch at each meal time. It took a couple of weeks until both cats felt comfortable enough to eat at the same time, separated by the closed door. With time, they progressed to playing together under the door, using a double-ended toy.

Roberta then moved the feeding stations away from the door, putting Iris's feeding station in the center of the sanctuary room, and moving Daisy's feeding station down the hall. Irresistible food was fed to both of them while the door to the room remained open. Everything went according to plan, with Roberta increasing the time the door was left open after the meals by one second at each feeding. After about one week, Roberta had a momentary fright. Iris ate, then made a dash out the door and toward Daisy. Daisy responded by lightly touching Iris's nose and nonchalantly sauntering past Roberta and into Iris's room to finish off Iris's dinner.

CHAPTER 6

Get Serious about Aggression

Aggression comes in a variety of types and intensities. It can range from a kitten struggling with boundaries to serious bites that send people to emergency rooms. Aggression can be more of a challenge to work with than some other unwelcome behaviors because there are many different kinds of aggression, and it is sometimes difficult to identify the cause or causes of the aggression. In some cases, aggressive behaviors are caused by underlying medical conditions or neurological problems. Taking your cat to your veterinarian for a checkup is very important for ruling out medical conditions or neurological problems that may be the basis of the aggression.

THE AGGRESSION SOLUTION TOOL KIT

- Primary reinforcer (treats)
- Secondary reinforcer (clicker)
- Fishing-pole toy and other cat-safe toys
- Vertical territory (cat trees, shelves, other high places)

Before you can modify medically related aggression successfully, the underlying medical conditions need to be addressed. Additionally, depending on the severity and circumstances of the aggression, consulting with either a certified cat-behavior consultant through the International Association of Animal Behavior Consultants or a veterinary behaviorist, who is well versed in cat behavior, can help identify the causes of the aggression and resolve the behavioral challenges.

Some examples of the kinds of aggression that cats can exhibit are pain-induced aggression, play aggression, status aggression, fear aggression, petting-induced aggression, maternal aggression, redirected aggression, intercat aggression, idiopathic aggression, and predatory aggression.

> ## A FEW DOS AND DON'TS OF AGGRESSION
>
> - **DON'T** pick up an aggressive cat.
> - **DON'T** use your hands to separate aggressive cats or put yourself between fighting cats.
> - **DON'T** punish an aggressive cat. Punishment can escalate the behavior and damages the cat–human bond.
> - **DO** be aware of warning signals by observing the cat's body language and vocalizations. In the case of intercat aggression, try to separate the cats, if possible, before aggressive behavior occurs by diverting or distracting them using noise, toys thrown across their field of vision, or an object placed between them so that they can't see each other.
> - **DO** read the rest of the chapter for more tips on working with aggression.

Because dealing with the long list of types of aggression is beyond the scope of this book, this chapter will focus only on the causes of and some solutions for petting-induced aggression, play aggression, and intercat aggression.

Petting-Induced Aggression

Petting-induced aggression is an unpleasant surprise for the unlucky recipient. It seems to come out of nowhere, shattering what appears to be an idyllic and relaxed experience between the cat and her favorite person. A typical scenario for this startling aggression is the following: the cat is settled comfortably on her favorite human's lap. Both are enjoying their evening, watching TV, relaxing on the couch, or reading a book. The cat is being stroked by her person, when suddenly the cat bites with no obvious provocation.

Cats have their reasons for exhibiting petting-induced aggression. It's up to us to figure them out and then to manage or eliminate the triggers. The cat may have a sensitive spot that she doesn't want touched, or perhaps the stroking becomes too intense for her after awhile. Cats can also display petting-induced aggression when they are falling asleep and are startled awake by petting. Sometimes their instinctive response is to bite whoever happens to be petting them.

Management, counter conditioning, and clicker training can help stop petting-induced aggression behavior.

Most of the time, cats will give warnings before biting. From the cats' perspective, they are clearly communicating their intentions. It's our job to pay attention and stop petting them when they warn us. A cat communicates in a number of ways when she is contemplating biting the hand that pets her. Commonly, she will look at your hand or at you before she bites. She also shows her displeasure through thumping her tail, changing her body position, ceasing to purr, rotating her ears back, vocalizing unhappily, tensing her muscles, and twitching her skin. Don't ignore these signals! Respect the cat's wishes and stop petting her immediately.

INSTINCT: THE BITER AND THE BITTEN

When a cat hunts and catches prey, she bites down and holds her victim. As the potential meal struggles to escape, the cat will instinctively bite harder and deeper. The cat's job as a predator is to catch her meal and eat. The prey's job is to escape and live another day.

In the heat of the moment, when a cat bites, her instinct takes control. She is hardwired to hold on and bite deeper when the victim tries to escape. Unfortunately, this can result in a bite that punctures the skin, and it can be very serious.

It is very hard to not act like prey when a cat is biting. If possible, instead of pulling away, try relaxing in position and gently pushing toward the cat's mouth. Don't push hard; you don't want to hurt her. Typically, a cat will then release her bite.

Place treats and clickers around the house where you and your cat relax together.

Tuning In

A combination of management, desensitizing, patience, and clicker training can help cats accept and maybe eventually luxuriate in long petting sessions. You can increase the rate and speed of your success while minimizing your injuries by tuning into your cat's body language. At the first sign of potential aggression or anxiety from your cat, practice the art of non-action. Stop petting her and don't interact with her. It's that simple.

Be attentive and know your cat. Possibly, your cat has an area that is very sensitive or painful to touch. Your veterinarian can help determine if this is a medical issue or a simple annoyance issue. Use your judgment in managing the situation and make sure to address any possible medical causes. Avoid touching your cat's sensitive spots.

Clicking Nonaction

Before changing your cat's opinion about the petting experience, you and your cat need to be fully versed in the basics of clicker training. You should review the step-by-step instructions in basic clicker training and conditioning the secondary reinforcer (pairing the clicker with something positive) found in chapter 1. Because your cat is meeting your strokes with bites and scratches, it is fair to assume that she is not motivated by petting. Food or play most likely rocks her socks. Place treats, toys, and clickers in locations around the house where your cat enjoys relaxing with you. This way, you will be prepared and ready to work with her no matter where you are in the house.

Once your house is fully stocked with treats and clickers, you are ready to begin. Choose a quiet time when your cat is calm and there isn't a lot of noise or distractions around. Ideally, your cat is relaxing quietly next to you or on one of her favorite napping areas.

Baby steps are the key. Be aware of your cat's tolerance levels. It is safe to assume that because you are seeking help with petting-induced aggression, you unfortunately have firsthand experience with breaching your cat's petting threshold. Some cats tolerate and enjoy being stroked for an extended time before striking out; others will allow only one or two strokes before declaring war.

The first step toward amnesty starts at a level that the cat enjoys or is neutral about. If your cat allows only two strokes before becoming reactive, start by stroking her only once. If she is relaxed, mark the event toward the end of the stroke with a click and then give her a treat, placing the treat so that she can easily reach it without moving out of her comfortable position. Do not click if she is displaying any signs of discomfort, aggression, or nervousness.

Watch her body language, including muscle tension. It is very important that you do not reinforce any agitation or stress. If there are any signs of anxiety, don't click; instead, end the session and wait for her to be calm and relaxed before starting again. At the next session, start at a lower level of petting. It might take a couple of tries before you discover her petting tolerance. To sum it up: reinforce the absence of aggression.

Remember to place your cat's well-earned treat next to her so that she doesn't have to relocate to eat it. After she's inhaled the treat and has relaxed, stroke her again. This time, your hand might linger for half a second longer, or your stroke might cover a slightly larger area. If her response is positive or neutral, click her toward the end of the stroke and then treat her. Click only when she's calm. Don't rush the process. It will take several sessions until she stops attacking when she is being petted.

Don't be discouraged if your cat is improving and then, all of a sudden, your progress seems to come to a screeching halt. You might be pushing the envelope a little too quickly—asking too much from your cat in too short of a time—or she has reached a temporary intolerance plateau. With patience and work, plateaus can be overcome by starting over from a lower level that she's comfortable with. If she's fine with being stroked four times, start with two strokes, clicking and treating as before. Chapter 3 discusses in detail how to overcome plateaus.

Spice it up by varying the strokes, the length of time you leave your hand on the cat, and where you are petting her. You will know by your cat's response if you are asking too much from her in too short of a time. Don't forget to celebrate and mark the successes, even if they are tiny.

At the first sign of stress, aggression, or discomfort, stop interacting with your cat immediately.

It's a good idea to remain alert with cats who have a history of petting-induced aggression. Be aware of their limits, but keep working to counter-condition them through clicker training, positive reinforcement, and management.

Play Aggression: Boundary Issues

Some cats and kittens have boundary issues regarding playing. The most common boundary challenge revolves around play intensity. Cats with play-intensity challenges will bite and scratch their favorite people during or right after play sessions. Sometimes cats and kittens with play-aggression challenges will play and attack their people whenever the mood hits them, sometimes wrapping themselves around their favorite people's legs and arms as the people are relaxing or sometimes attacking late at night while their people sleep. It's all about boundaries—or lack thereof. Some cats and kittens with play-aggression issues were either taken from their mom and siblings at too young of an age or have human companions who have encouraged rough play by using their hands when playing. Other cats' play-aggression challenges are rooted in boredom. They don't have enough environmental stimulation or playtime.

Kittens learn important socialization skills from playing with their siblings and mom. When kittens play too roughly with each other, the kitten who is hurt will cry out, signaling her littermate to back off on the roughhousing. These play skills are boundary builders, teaching kittens about bite inhibition and when to turn the play down a notch or two.

Some adults and children have boundary issues when playing with cats and kittens. They use their hands when playing and they play too roughly. This is not a good idea. Using hands to play with a cat sends the message that it's OK for the cat to attack and bite hands or feet whenever the mood hits her. Gloves with toys hanging on them also send the wrong message to the cat. Cats are smart; they know that your hand is in the glove. For the same reasons, don't play with your cat with your hands and feet while they are under sheets and blankets. This sends the cat the wrong message about play. From the cat's perspective, it is hard to

Environmental enrichment, including toys and scratchers, will help keep cats interested, stimulated, and mentally challenged.

understand why it's sometimes OK to bite and scratch their favorite humans, but not OK at other times. Instead of using your hands when playing with your cat, use toys such as fishing-pole toys or little balls—just remember to keep your hand out of reach!

Timeouts

When your cat plays too roughly with you, don't yell or punish her. Instead, send her the message that this is not an OK way to play by giving her a timeout. A timeout for play aggression is simple and short. Just turn around, leave the room, and close the door behind you. Your cat will be surprised and startled that her victim, I mean, *playmate*, is no longer available to be mauled. It is important that you don't pick her up, utter any swear words, or engage her in any way at this time. Doing so will only reinforce the play aggression.

Timeouts are usually short; thirty seconds to a minute or two is usually all that is needed for play aggression. Come back after the timeout, and if she has calmed down, either continue playing at a less intense level using a toy, or do another, lower energy, activity with her. It can take a few timeouts until she starts to understand the play boundaries.

Work and Play

Schedule consistent daily play sessions with your cat and don't let them become intense. If she's a cat who likes to hang from the chandeliers and dance on the bookcases, consider having multiple sessions every day with her. Older, calmer cats ideally should have two daily play sessions. Good times for play sessions are morning and evening. These are the times that most cats are the most active and eager to play. Don't forget to cater to her natural instincts by imitating the hunt.

Provide your cat with lots of environmental enrichment and interactive toys to play with. Almost anything can become a cat toy. Paper bags without handles and wadded-up pieces of paper are examples of spontaneously made toys that

> ### WEAPONS READY
>
> Fluffy may look sweet rolling around, exposing her little stomach to you. It can be hard to resist petting that adorable tummy! Be aware that when a cat is on her back, all weapons are ready to be deployed. Many cats have an automatic response of grabbing, kicking, and/or biting hands and arms when their stomachs are being tickled or petted. Some cats seem to enjoy having their little stomachs rubbed and petted, but be aware that those idyllic moments can change instantaneously.

PLAY TIME

I find Pam Johnson-Bennett's play techniques, as outlined in her book *Starting from Scratch*, very effective for dispersing cat energy. Use a fishing-pole toy and pretend that the toy at the end is prey. Make the chase challenging by pulling the toy under the sofa or inside a paper bag. The toy should run and stop in spits and spurts, just like prey in the field. Because prey animals never run toward their pursuer, don't pull the toy back toward the cat. The goal is to work the cat and get her very involved with the game.

When you're ready to stop playing, don't just stop. Instead, slow the toy down. Pretend that the toy on the end of the pole is tired or wounded, gradually moving slower. Finally, let your cat catch it one last time. Immediately after she catches it, feed her something delicious. This could be her regular meal or a scrumptious treat. She will eat, groom, and then go to sleep a happy, mighty hunter. Remember to put the fishing pole out of reach when you're not around to supervise the play.

can provide hours of entertainment for cats. Even dog toys can make good cat toys. Just make sure that the toys are safe for the cat. Some of my favorites are puzzle toys that make cats work a little for their treats. One such toy has separate compartments that are covered by sliders. In order for the cat to access the food, she has to move the sliders to open the compartments. Another puzzle toy is made of hollowed-out plastic dog bones positioned on top of each other. The cat has to spin each dog bone in order to reach the food. A favorite toy among cats is a versatile toy-scratcher combination. It's flat and circular in shape, with a cardboard scratcher in the middle that is surrounded by a channel that contains a ball. Treats and other toys can be hidden in the channel along with the ball.

Clicker Play

Clicker training and clicker play will help stop play aggression by directing the cat's energy toward something other than your hand or leg. Needless to say, your cat must have basic clicker skills; she should be target-trained and able to sit on request. Clicking is a fun way to channel her hyper-play energy and will mentally challenge her. Put some of her play actions on cue. For instance, if she's a jumper, use clicker training to capture a jump with a click, followed by a treat. The time to do this is before she becomes overstimulated.

Your cat will appreciate daily play sessions. Always use toys when playing and monitor the sessions so they don't become too intense.

Start by having your cat sit on request (the process for teaching your cat to sit is described in chapter 2). Always begin her jump behavior with a *sit* request so that the behavior has a beginning, setting it apart from her other energetic activities. Once she's sitting, use the target stick or a feather wand to encourage her to jump by holding it up above her. While she jumps, click; when she lands, give her a treat. After she performs this behavior correctly eight out of ten times when cued for it with the target or feather wand, hang a verbal cue on it. As you lure her with the wand, say the

A CAUSE FOR FRUSTRATION

I don't recommend playing with cats using laser pointers. Besides the danger of accidentally shining it in a cat's eye (which can damage the eye), laser-pointer play is frustrating and unproductive for a cat. It may appear that cats love to chase the disappearing dot, but the pleasure of the chase is quickly replaced with frustration because they can never have the satisfaction of capturing their prey.

Play is an extension of hunting. The capture is a very important component of both. Cats love the feel of freshly caught prey (a toy) under their paws. Laser pointers don't provide that feeling of satisfaction that comes with the capture. Instead, cats become frustrated and drive themselves crazy trying to catch that elusive laser dot. No matter how hard they try, they will never catch it.

word "jump." You can take it a few steps further, teaching her to jump through hoops, through your arms, or even into your arms on request. Chapter 9 has instructions for different tricks that you can teach your cat.

Timing is important. Don't clicker-train your cat when she is aggressive or overstimulated. Clicking during those times will reinforce the aggressive behavior. Timeouts, as described earlier in this chapter, are called for when she is play-biting or play-scratching.

Your cat can also be taught to run an agility course, which will expend a lot of energy. You can set up the course in your living room and train your cat to weave through poles and run through tunnels or over ladders. Chairs on their sides, small ladders, tunnels, plastic cones, and boxes to navigate around and over are examples of some homemade cat agility equipment. Train her to navigate the course using either a target or a feather wand to lure her through it. Make sure to click and treat her when she successfully negotiates each obstacle. Cat agility has become very popular at cat shows, and an organization called International Cat Agility Tournaments (ICAT) provides guidance to enthusiasts wanting to start their own agility groups.

If possible, schedule your clicker sessions at the same times every day. The best times are right before your cat's regular play sessions. These training sessions will mentally challenge her, give her something to look forward to, and delight her because she is having fun with her favorite person.

Play is an extension of the hunt. Help keep your cat's frustration level down by allowing her to periodically catch her toy.

Commercially available puzzle toys and other interactive cat toys, such as ball-and-track toys, will help keep your cat occupied and challenged.

Intercat Aggression

There are many possible causes for intercat aggression, but usually it involves a cat or cats between the ages of two and four years who have reached social maturity. Not unlike human adolescents, cats go through a time in which they are trying to figure out their place in the world and how they fit in with those around them. Intercat aggression can be alarming, especially when it occurs between cats who used to get along well with each other. Most commonly, intercat aggression is displayed between two males, although females, depending on the circumstances, can also engage in this often-violent behavior. Intercat aggression can also be caused by social hierarchy issues, unknown cats, fear, and territorial challenges.

Displays of intercat aggression can range from passive aggression to violent active aggression, and can include all of the types in between. Modifying the behavior is contingent upon the cause and the degree of the aggression. Management combined with behavior modification and clicker training, along with time and patience, can help change the cats' attitudes toward each other so that they will at least tolerate each other. Spaying/neutering is also part of the solution if your cats are whole. If the aggression is severe, reintroducing the cats to each other with the procedure outlined in chapter 5 can resolve the problem. Occasionally, there are situations in which the only way to restore peace and harmony is to find a wonderful new home for one of the warring cats, but exhaust all of your options before resorting to this sad solution.

Intercat aggression can occur between two newly introduced cats as well as between cats who previously got along with each other.

The Importance of Vertical Spaces

Cats who are similar in status or who are trying to figure out their places in the world are more apt to quarrel when they do not have other ways to work out their hierarchy. Tall cat trees, window perches, shelving systems, bookcases, and other tall furniture pieces are just what the cat ordered to peacefully display social hierarchy, so provide plenty of high places with different levels. Cats demonstrate status by how high they sit in comparison with other animals in the household. The hierarchy is not static. It is dynamic and dependent on many factors, including the time of day, the room, and the cats. You may find that one cat is at the top of the cat tree every morning, yet another cat occupies the same position at noon.

Tall cat trees, book shelves, perches, and other furniture can provide the vertical territory that cats need.

The configuration of the furniture and shelves is important. Be careful not to accidentally set up a situation where cats can feel trapped. Aggressive behavior sometimes occurs when there is only one way up and down from a high area; the cat coming down might meet the cat going up, resulting in swatting and hissing. Avoid this by providing multiple routes up and down. Positioning cat trees next to other pieces of furniture such as bookshelves, window perches, and other cat trees can also help provide multiple routes up and down from the tops of cat trees. Location is important, too. The cat furniture, shelves, and perches should be located where the cats like to hang out, which is usually in the rooms where their favorite humans spend time.

NOT ALL CAT TREES ARE CREATED EQUAL

When investing in a cat tree, be aware that not all cat trees are created equal. The best kinds of cat trees are those that are tall, with sturdy bases and wide shelves. The shelves should not be stacked on top of each other. It is very important that the shelf configuration doesn't set up a situation where a cat can be trapped at the top of the tree. Cat trees should discourage, not encourage, aggression. Avoid confrontations by ensuring there are multiple ways up and down the tree.

Due Diligence

Be observant and look for trends. For instance, some cats get cranky during specific times, such as mornings and evenings; other cats display aggression in specific locations. If you see a time or place correlation to aggressive behavior, keep the cats separated from each other in those situations until the problem is resolved.

In cases of severe aggression, when the cats can't be in the same room without declaring war, separate them and slowly reintroduce them to each other. Keep in mind that separation should never be a punishment. Make sure that all of the cats have food, water, comfortable places to sleep, environmental enrichment, and, if possible, a secure window to look out of.

In cases of relatively mild to medium displays of aggression, supervise the cats when they are in the same room. Allow them to mingle during the inactive times—the times when they are usually the most sedate. These mellow times provide good opportunities for encouraging better attitudes and building better relationships with the help of clicker training.

CAT SCOUT CLICKER MOTTO: BE PREPARED

Make sure that you always have a clicker and treats with you, or place them in strategic areas throughout the house. That way, you will be ready to mark the positive behaviors when they occur.

Reinforce your cats when they are together and not displaying any signs of anxiety or aggression.

Click Those Troubles Away

Again, before clicking away intercat aggression, the cats need to know a few clicker-training principles. Don't stop with the basics. Teaching your cats to sit and stay on their respective mats or chairs as described in chapters 1 through 3 will help down the road in encouraging your cats to call a permanent truce.

Cats who are very cranky and can't seem to ever coexist in a room without becoming violent or uttering nasty words at each other will probably need to start from the beginning. Pretend they are strangers and formally reintroduce them to each other as outlined in chapter 5. Because the cats have an unpleasant history with each other, it may take more time and clicks until they will even tolerate each other.

Many cats have milder forms of intercat aggression. They can usually be together for short periods of time without trying to kill each other or having words. Be equally aware of their down times as you are of their hissy fits, and make a note of the locations where the temporary ceasefires occur. Take advantage of the suspension of hostilities by clicking and treating the cats when they are peaceful while together in the same room or casually passing each other in the hall. Click and treat only if there are no signs of aggression, potential aggression, or anxiety. Click only once and then immediately reward both cats, tossing a treat first to the cat who is either the most aggressive or the most food-aggressive, then tossing a treat to the other cat. Timing is important. It's crucial to mark the truces with a click as they are happening, not one second before or after.

Remember, relationships aren't built in a day. Be patient and consistent. The cats will eventually expand their ceasefire zones to other locations and times. When you find the cats spending more time together without incident, you can push the envelope and clicker-train them together.

The cats need to be well schooled in clicker training basics, sitting, and staying on request. Work with both

Position yourself between the cats and direct the cues, reinforcement, and rewards toward the cat you are working with.

cats when they are relaxing in the same room at the same time. Their individual stools, chairs, or props they perform on need to be placed in the room at a comfortable distance from each other. The distance depends on the cats themselves. If they peacefully coexist 10 feet from each other, then place the stools or chairs 10 feet apart. If your cats need more space or if their line of demarcation is closer, adjust their chairs or stools accordingly.

Start the training by cuing the more aggressive cat to stand, sit, and then stay on her stool. Of course, click and treat when she does as requested. While she is staying, request the same behavior from your other cat. When work-

Be aware of both cats' body language. At the first sign of agitation or loss of interest in clicker training, safely separate them.

ing with multiple cats, stand between the two cats, partially obstructing the cats' view of each other. Position yourself next to the cat you are working with and direct your attention and the clicker toward her when you click.

Be aware of both cats' tolerance levels. In order to be effective, clicker train-ing needs to be fun for everyone. If one cat gets bored or becomes agitated, simply stop the session for both cats, nonchalantly and safely separate them, and begin another session a few hours later or the next day. Once the cats will work together, gradually decrease the space between their stools by one half of an inch each session. If there are any signs of agitation or if the cats go on strike, slow down. You are proceeding too quickly, and you need to go back to the origi-nal safe distance. Remember 300 Peck Pigeon in chapter 3?

If your cats refuse to work together, continue each cat's education by teach-ing new behaviors while the two are separated. Remember, even when cats do their clicker-training exercises side by side, it's important to separate them when-ever teaching new behaviors so they do not distract each other. After the new behaviors are learned separately, the cats can practice them in the same room, each on her own stool or chair. The goal is that eventually the cats can declare a truce and be together without aggression.

Case Study: Intercat Aggression

SITUATION: Leo, Mars, Athena, and Venus were spayed and neutered cats who were between three and four years old. They've all lived with Joe and Angie since they were kittens. The four cats had been friends until recently, when the two boys started fighting with each other. The brawls always started the same way, with Leo attacking Mars. Mars had become frightened and developed litter-box issues, urinating directly outside the litter-box room. According to Angie, Mars spent most of his time nervously looking over his shoulder. The aggression appeared to be worse in the mornings and evenings. There were times when they could be in the same room together without incident, although those times seemed few and far between, especially because Mars spent much of his time hiding under the bed. Joe and Angie were heartbroken. These two boys used to be best friends.

Angie, Joe, and the four cats lived in a 1200-square-foot home. The cats had three litter boxes, all located in the TV room. The tallest pieces of furniture in the house were sofas and desks.

ASSESSMENT: The two boys, who had reached the age of social maturity, were trying to figure out their place in the hierarchy. Because the home was small and without vertical territory, the two males couldn't work out their positions in the household through physical positioning in their environment. Instead, they were fighting in an effort to establish the hierarchy. Additionally, there weren't enough litter boxes, and the three boxes that were provided for the cats were located in the same room. Mars did not feel secure enough to use them because of Leo's attacks, so he resorted to urinating outside the litter-box area.

RECOMMENDATIONS: I recommended a combination of environmental changes, management, and clicker training. Joe and Angie added three tall cat trees and two shelves to provide vertical territory for the cats. The trees were placed in the TV room, the bedroom, and the living room—the places that Joe and Angie spent most of their time when they were home. They added perches and shelves in the kitchen and dining room. High shelves near the ceiling were added, allowing the cats to navigate easily between the cat trees. They worked well, providing additional places high up for the cats. The addition of the vertical territory eased the aggression by a considerable amount, allowing Leo to show his status by his physical positioning. The couple added two large, uncovered litter boxes in different areas of the house, allowing all of the cats to have more choices.

It took about twenty minutes for Angie to clicker-train both Mars and Leo, separately, to the point of both cats having strong positive associations with the sound of the clicker. Angie placed clickers and treats in little plastic containers throughout the house.

Initially, the cats were only allowed to mingle together in the afternoon, when there were typically fewer aggressive incidents. Joe and Angie supervised the cats at all times during these visits. Sometimes, Leo would still stalk Mars. Angie, recognizing the body language, immediately blocked Leo's view of Mars so that Mars could escape without incident. When the two cats were relaxed in the same room, Angie marked the absence of aggression with one click, immediately followed with two treats, tossing Leo his treat a fraction of a second before Mars got his. Angie noted that, after about one week, both cats were spending more time in the room together with fewer incidents. She continued to mark these peaceful times by clicking once and tossing the treats to the cats. One month after the work began, the two cats sat on the same cat tree together, Leo on the top shelf, Mars on the lower shelf.

The relationship between Leo and Mars improved to the point that the cats could be together in the same room without trying to kill each other. They were never again best buddies, but at least they tolerated each other.

Trauma-Free Carriers and Vet Visits

Transporting to and visiting the veterinarian can be very traumatizing for everyone involved, including cats, their people, and veterinarians. Chasing a cat around the house to deposit her, screaming and protesting, into a carrier is not the best way to start the excursion. Maybe the experience is accompanied by the cat's hiding and objecting—the only way the cat knows how to communicate her viewpoint about the carrier. Listening to the cat loudly voice her complaints while navigating traffic will increase the anxiety level of even the most passive person.

THE VET-VISIT TOOL KIT
- Primary reinforcer (treats)
- Secondary reinforcer (clicker)
- Hard-sided carrier
- Puppy pads/small towels
- Synthetic pheromone spray
- Large towel

Then there's the vet visit itself. Some cats are so frightened that they metamorphose into either Cujo kitties or a traumatized little bundle of fur, huddling in the corners of their carriers. There is a kinder, gentler way to take cats to the vet. Cats can be acclimated to their carriers, the car ride, and the vet experience through clicker training and counter-conditioning/ desensitizing.

Solving Carrier Avoidance

You may be living with a cat who will do anything in her power to avoid getting near a carrier. Your cat may be one of those disappearing cats who, at the slightest hint that there might be a carrier in the room, will hide for days, only tentatively venturing out for food and water when no human is in sight. Or you may have a clinging cat who clinches all four paws onto the carrier sides, making it impossible to lower her into the carrier, or a kitty who latches onto anything or anyone in order to avoid that evil carrier.

CARRIER WARNING

Always check the doors and latches of your carrier before picking it up. Make sure that the latches, screws, and other closures are secured firmly in the locked position before lifting the carrier. A loose latch can result in the carrier's coming apart and your cat's being released wherever you happen to be at the time. Carrier doors also need to be checked. They can accidentally be placed incorrectly when assembling the carrier, resulting in their opening or falling off at an inopportune time.

The cat's traumatic association with the carrier needs to be changed to be more positive, or at least neutral. This is important for vet trips and for possible crises, such as a house fire. Emergencies and other unexpected events can occur, making it vital that cats go willingly and quickly into their carriers. Even if there isn't an emergency, who wants to spend hours chasing a cat through the house in order to wrestle her into the carrier?

The Carrier

I recommend a hard carrier because the top comes off, making it easier to access the cat. Some hard carriers have latches; others use large screws to fasten the pieces together. At least one model has multiple openings, one of which is located on the top. The carrier needs to be large enough for your cat to comfortably stand up and turn around in. There should also be enough room to

Hard-sided carriers can be quickly taken apart, making it less stressful and easier for the veterinarian to examine your cat.

add absorbent pads (like those used for house-training puppies) or a soft towel on the bottom of the carrier; to make it more inviting to the cat.

A Carrier by Any Other Name

It may be hard to believe that you can change your cat's opinion of the carrier so that she doesn't perceive it as an evil place. Start by taking your carrier apart. Unlatch the top and remove the doors. Place the bottom of the carrier in one of your cat's favorite locations. It should be left there for a few weeks, maybe even a couple of months.

Place something soft that already has your cat's scent on it on the carrier bottom. A towel that the cat has been sleeping on will work, or you can gently pet your cat with a towel and then place it in the carrier. Pillows or an article of clothing she likes to sleep on will also work. It doesn't matter what you use as long as it's comfortable for your cat to sit or sleep on and it smells like her.

Before you can change your cat's opinion of the carrier, she will need to have the basic clicker-training skills that are described in chapter 1.

The carrier bottom should become a comfortable, fun place for the cat to go.

Carrier = Fun

You can start to change your cat's perception of the carrier through clicker training. When your cat happens to walk by the bottom portion of the carrier, mark the event with a click and a treat. Click and treat her whenever there is either a positive or neutral interaction with the carrier. Nonchalantly sauntering past the bottom part of the carrier, or sitting next to or inside of it deserves recognition. Throw the treat into the carrier bottom after you click so that she has to go into the carrier to eat it. Because every cat is an individual with her own schedule, it's impossible to gauge how long it will take until she decides the carrier is an OK place, maybe even a friendly place, to spend time. It may take a day, or it could take a week or longer. It's up to the cat. If your cat isn't too big on treats, use her regular food as a reward. You might want to time the carrier sessions so that they occur just before her usual mealtimes.

Play can also help change her carrier perceptions. Use the fishing-pole toy, dragging it into and around the carrier. When she chases the toy into the carrier bottom, toss a small treat in the carrier for her. Some cats love to play fetch. If you are lucky enough to share your world with a cat who fetches, toss the toy into the carrier for her. When she goes in, toss a treat to her while she's in the carrier. Your cat might prefer other activities over play. She may enjoy being brushed, or she might be motivated by affection. Whatever activities she enjoys, do them around and in the carrier as much as possible.

Topping It Off

Once your kitty is comfortable going inside the bottom part of the carrier, put the top of the carrier back in place without installing the door. Make sure to check that the top is securely fastened, because if it moves or falls, the sound and movement could startle your cat and cause her to be more frightened around the carrier. At this stage of the carrier-introduction process, the door remains removed so that your cat can go in and out as she pleases and therefore doesn't feel trapped.

Continue the activities you started when the top was off of the carrier, always throwing the treat inside the carrier. Additionally, when playing with her, throw her toys into the carrier. When she chases her toys into the carrier, click (only if she's inside) and toss a treat to her.

Cats who fall into the Foodie category mentioned in chapter 2 enjoy treasure hunts. Hide treats throughout the house on cat trees, on shelves, on bookcases, in toys, and in the carrier. The cat carrier is a perfect location to hide treats for her to find.

Don't forget to click and treat your cat if she just happens to be inside the carrier of her own volition. The goal is for her to lose her fear of the carrier and see it as either a neutral location or a place where fun things happen. Don't feel discouraged if your cat doesn't go into the carrier. Some cats take weeks until they feel comfortable enough to

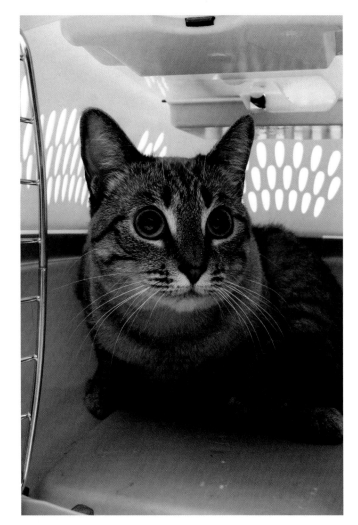

Don't force your cat to go into the carrier. Take your time and help her learn to have positive associations with the carrier.

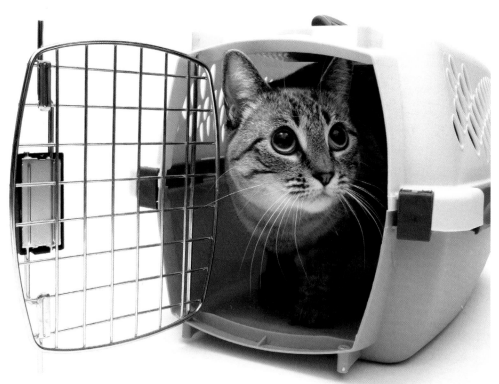

Install the carrier door and leave it open. Continue to play and clicker train your cat in the carrier. Close the door only after she's comfortable.

go inside their carriers on a regular basis; others change their perceptions and feelings about the carriers more quickly. It is important that you don't force your cat inside the carrier; forcing her will reinforce her fears about carriers. Instead, gently motivate her by engaging her in activities she enjoys around the carrier and through clicker training.

The Carrier Door

Once your cat is comfortable going in and out of the carrier, reinstall the door. Continue all of the activities and training, making sure that the door is always open. It needs to stay open until she's used to going into the carrier. When she's comfortable with the arrangement, close the door after she's gone in. Leave it closed for about one second and then open it. Make sure to click your cat and give her a really yummy treat, pushing it through the bars on the door when she's in the carrier with the door closed. The next time your cat goes into the carrier, increase the time the door is closed by one second. If your cat is uncomfortable or nervous, immediately back off. You are asking too much too fast from her and you need to go back to a stage where she's in her comfort zone. Proceed at a slower pace.

The Pick Up

The challenges can be increased only after your cat is calm while inside the carrier with the door closed for about five minutes. After she passes the calm test, carefully pick the carrier up and then gently put it down. Face the carrier door toward you so that you can see her response. If she's OK in the carrier while you hold it up, click her. After putting the carrier back on the floor, open the carrier and toss a treat in for her. Leave the carrier door open so that she can come and go as she pleases. Leaving the door open will help her feel in control; she can eat the treat and either leave or stay in the carrier, whatever she chooses.

Gradually increase the time and distance that you move the carrier while she's in it. At first, move the

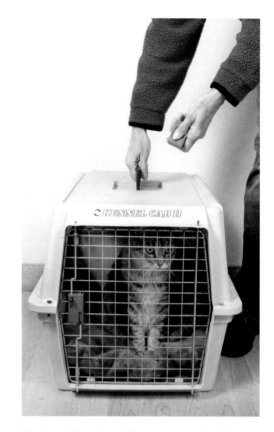

If your cat is calm while you are moving her in the carrier, click once, put down the carrier, and then give her a treat.

SPRITZ TO CALM

Synthetic pheromone sprays are available that are similar to the synthetic pheromone diffusers that are plugged into the wall (discussed in chapter 8). These mimic the friendly pheromones that cats produce from scent glands located on their cheeks and can help take the edge off stressful situations, including the trip to the vet. One or two quick sprays inside the carrier is all that is needed. Wait about twenty minutes before encouraging your cat to go into the carrier.

Ask your veterinarian and the vet tech to spray one spritz of the pheromone spray onto their hands before handling your cat. One quick spray on the hands, with the hands rubbed together and air-dried for a couple of minutes, will help take the edge off the stress for some cats before being handled.

Keep in mind that these synthetic pheromone sprays are not magic bullets. They need to be used along with all of the other recommendations.

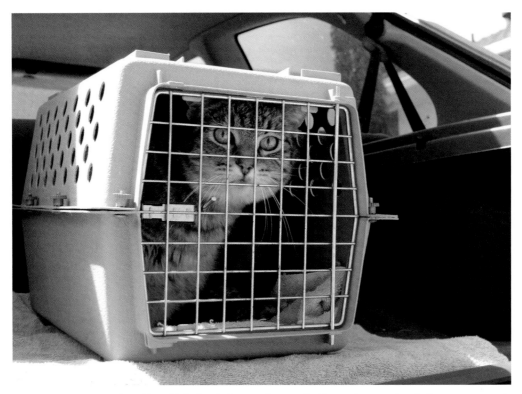

After your cat is comfortable with being in her carrier, gradually get her used to being transported in a car.

carrier only a few feet. If she is calm and displaying no signs of anxiety, click while you are moving her and then put the carrier down, open the door, and toss a yummy treat in to her. Soon, you should be able to pick up the carrier with her in it and carry her into another room. Make sure you click and treat her for her bravery.

Continue to work with her until you can comfortably carry her around the whole house in the carrier. At any sign of discomfort or stress, stop, put her down, and let her out of the carrier in a safe location. Go back to an earlier stage where she was comfortable, and proceed more slowly from there.

The Car

Cars can be scary places for cats. Unfortunately, most veterinary visits mean trips in the car. After your cat is comfortable with being carried around your home in the carrier, you can start to prepare her for car trips. Before taking your cat to the car while she's in the carrier, double-check to make sure that the carrier is securely fastened.

Make the situation a little easier for your cat by covering her carrier with a towel so that the sounds and sights of the great outdoors are less invasive and scary. Before taking her out to the car, clear off a spot on the back seat for the carrier. Once you've placed the towel and cleared a spot, your cat is ready for her first driving lesson.

Put the carrier with your cat in it in the car, sit next to her, and close the door. Click and push the treat through the openings in the carrier door when your cat is calm, displaying no stress or anxiety. It is natural for some cats to display anxiety and fear during the car experience. If your cat is extremely frightened and is huddling in the corner of the carrier or loudly vocalizing, take her back to the house and proceed through the steps again, but this time, take more time during each of the phases.

Turn the car on, and if the cat is calm, take her on a short trip down the driveway. Then bring her back into the house and let her out of the carrier. Have multiple sessions over a few days or a week, gradually increasing the time she's in the car.

TRANSPORTING MAULEE

Maulee, my fifteen-year-old Bengal, took a terrible fall that resulted in her having major surgery to repair a serious laceration. Tragically, on the same day of Maulee's accident, my father died. Because being with my family and caring for Maulee after her surgery were both priorities, I had to bring Maulee to my mom's house every day in order to medicate her and keep her injury clean, which meant daily trips in the carrier and car.

Maulee has no problems with carriers and is very good about going into them. In fact, she loves her carrier. She has always hated the car experience though, or so I thought. Her usual reaction was to scream and howl at the top of her lungs throughout the whole journey. I now know why.

Maulee loves dehydrated chicken. It occurred to me while I was driving with one hand on the wheel and stuffing chicken through the carrier door with the other that I was reinforcing her yelling. Every time she yelled, she got a piece of chicken. Maulee had quickly learned how to get her favorite treat hand-delivered. All she had to do was holler for it.

I changed her behavior by getting into the back of the car with her, armed with dehydrated chicken. She was screaming, as usual. She did have to breathe, though. When she stopped to take a breath, I took advantage of the momentary silence by immediately clicking and giving her a treat. The pauses between the screams became longer. She soon figured out that when she was quiet, she was reinforced with a click and rewarded with a treat.

The Visit to the Veterinarian

Congratulations! You and your kitty both deserve delicious treats because your cat now accepts the carrier and can be transported without trauma to the veterinarian's office. The next hurdle is the actual vet visit. Some cats are terrified of veterinary clinics. Unfortunately, if your cat previously had a bad experience at the veterinarian's, then subsequent visits to the vet can be increasingly difficult for her, you, and the veterinarian.

There are a few things that you and the veterinary staff can do to minimize the trauma and make the visit to the clinic as stress-free as possible for everyone involved.

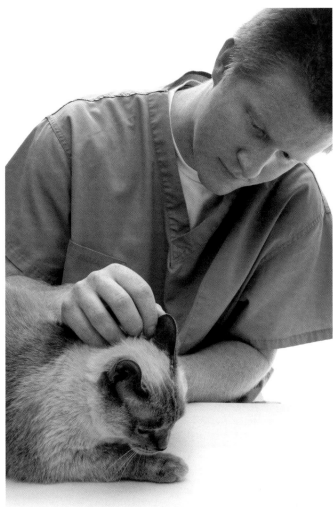

Now that your cat feels comfortable with the carrier, you can continue to use clicker training to make her trip to the vet less stressful.

The Waiting Room

Usually, you have to cool your heels in the waiting room for what feels like an eternity before the veterinarian can see you. The towel should still be covering your cat's carrier to shelter her from the noises and sights of the clinic. Covering the carrier will also give her the sense of being hidden from harm. If you do have to wait, try to find a quiet place to sit that is away from the other animal visitors. Position the carrier so that your cat can't see the other patients at the clinic. If your cat responds positively to your voice in stressful situations, she may appreciate you talking quietly to her, reassuring her with your voice.

The Examination Room

After you are escorted into the examination room, remove the towel from the carrier and spread it out on the examination table. In addition to making the hard table a little friendlier, your cat will recognize the towel's smell when she is removed from the carrier, possibly taking a little of the edge off the stress.

It can be challenging for the veterinary technician or veterinarian to examine a cat who is huddled in a corner of the carrier. Scruffing (grabbing the cat by the loose skin at the back of her neck) and pulling a cat out of the carrier could potentially traumatize the cat and result in bites and scratches, making the vet experience terrifying for everyone involved. The cat-removal process can be made gentler by using the top-down approach. If possible, before the veterinarian comes into the exam room, unlatch the carrier top, but don't remove it. This way, the cat will feel safe for as long as possible. When the vet is ready to examine your cat, the carrier top can be easily lifted off.

An added bonus to this examination approach is that, depending on the circumstances and the cat, the veterinarian can sometimes partially examine the cat while she is still in the familiar carrier, making the exam a little less stressful for everyone.

Your cat will respond better if the veterinarian and his assistant get to know your cat before they handle her. You can start the introductions by telling your veterinarian a little about the cat and her symptoms. Also, if you know the cat has sensitive spots, is prone to scratching people she doesn't know, or hangs from the ceiling when stressed, let the veterinarian know. Additionally, your vet will appreciate knowing if your cat is strong or if she has mastered the fine art of twisting out of a person's hands.

Most cats will respond favorably to this calm approach, but as with everything in life, there is always the exception. Some of these exceptional cats can be patiently worked with so that they are not as anxious at the clinic; others are severely traumatized by the experience. If you have a kitty who is terrified by vet visits, discuss with your vet all of the options, including home visits and veterinarian-prescribed medications for making the visit as stress-free as possible.

REASSURANCE

Reassure your cat when she's in her carrier by placing something that smells like you with her in the carrier. A pillowcase from the pillow you slept on the night before or an old T-shirt you recently slept in will help reassure her during her trip.

Your veterinarian will appreciate your telling him about your cat's personality and her usual response in stressful situations.

Honey, We're Home!

Cats smell strange to other cats after a trip to the veterinarian. They smell like the clinic. We humans don't notice this, but the cats who stayed home do. They recognize their friend visually, but she sure smells weird. This can result in confusion, confrontation, and sometimes violence between cats. Neither you nor your cat needs the additional stress after the exciting visit to the veterinarian.

When your cat arrives home from the vet, put her in a separate room to avoid confrontation. Use a clean towel to gently massage the cat who stayed home, then massage the cat who was at the vet with the same towel. The mutual towel massage will transfer the smell of the stay-at-home companion cat onto the other cat, helping the cat who stayed home recognize her old friend.

When your cat comes home from the veterinarian, use a clean towel to transfer the stay-at-home cat's scent onto the cat who went to the clinic.

Case Study: Jinniyha at the Veterinarian

SITUATION: A couple of years ago, on a cold winter's day, Jinniyha, one of my Bengal girls, was very sick and needed immediate veterinary help. Naturally, she was sick on a Sunday night; because my regular veterinarian was not available, we had to go to an emergency vet. I put Jinniyha in her hard-sided carrier and put the carrier in the back seat of my car, and off we drove.

After we arrived at the clinic, we were ushered into a small exam room. A vet tech came in to do the preliminary exam. The vet tech didn't say much as I struggled to unlatch the top of the carrier so that Jinniyha could be lifted out. Because it was a cold night, my fingers weren't working as fast or adeptly as they could have been, and I had trouble unsnapping a couple of the latches. The vet tech ignored my request for help, and instead sighed in exasperation and opened the front door of the carrier. She reached in to scruff Jinniyha and drag her out of the carrier by her neck. This was a fatal error for the vet tech. The vet tech knew nothing about Jinniyha, nor did she ask. Jinniyha's immediate response was to bite the vet tech and escape out of the carrier, propelling herself to the highest spot she could find, which just happened to be the top of my head.

The vet tech yelled at me and ran out to bandage her hand. Meanwhile, I untangled Jinniyha's claws from my scalp, peeled her off my head, and comforted her in my sweater as she trembled and shook.

ASSESSMENT: Jinniyha responded to both the insensitive handling by the vet tech and not feeling well by displaying fear-based behavior.

SOLUTION: A couple of minutes later, the vet walked in and started to talk softly to Jinniyha and ask me questions; then he extended his index finger for her to sniff. She relaxed. The vet then examined her with no problem whatsoever. What a difference the right approach and handling can make.

This experience that Jinniyha and I had on that cold winter's day was the inspiration for this chapter.

8

Cats with Bathroom Issues

One of the most frustrating cat-behavior challenges we encounter is inappropriate elimination. The sad news is that it's one of the top reasons for cats' being surrendered to shelters and subsequently euthanized. The good news is that, in the majority of cases, this problem can be solved. Sometimes the solutions are easy fixes; other cases may take a little more work and time. Our little cat companions are worth the extra work that it may take to fix the problem and keep them at home, not surrendered to a local shelter.

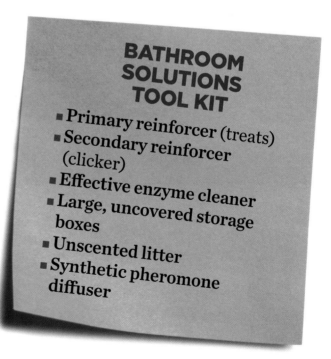

BATHROOM SOLUTIONS TOOL KIT

- Primary reinforcer (treats)
- Secondary reinforcer (clicker)
- Effective enzyme cleaner
- Large, uncovered storage boxes
- Unscented litter
- Synthetic pheromone diffuser

Cats always have reasons for their behavior. When they have litter-box issues, it's not their fault and they shouldn't be punished for it. They are responding to something in their environment, a medical problem, or events that have been or are occurring in their world. Cats don't wake up one day after a nap and randomly decide to urinate on the sofa, nor do they think out of the blue that it would be fun to wander over and spray the door. Poor litter-box management is the most typical reason behind litter-box issues, and that is easy for us to correct. Additionally, it is common for cats who have not been altered to respond to the call of the wild by spraying and eliminating outside their litter boxes.

As with all unappreciated behaviors, the causes of the behavior need to be identified so that they can be addressed and the behavior stopped through a combination of management, environmental changes, and behavior modification.

Medical and Hormonal Triggers

Before determining that this is a behavioral problem, take your cat to a veterinarian. The vet visit has to be at the top of the list because some medical conditions that cause cats to eliminate outside their litter boxes can be life-threatening and very painful. Some of the potentially responsible medical conditions and diseases include urinary-tract infections, diabetes, kidney disease, thyroid disease, and senility, but the complete list is endless. And don't forget defecation outside of the litter box. Constipation, parasites, diarrhea, and inflammatory bowel disease are just a few medical problems that can cause cats to defecate outside their boxes. I can't stress enough how important it is to have your cat checked by a veterinarian.

The Birds and the Bees

Hormones can be a major factor in inappropriate urination, so be sure to have your cats spayed or neutered. Both whole males and whole females commonly spray and sometimes won't use their boxes. These hot-and-bothered cats are leaving their calling cards for other cats. Putting them in neutral by spaying or neutering them will usually solve the problem. After altering, it takes about one month for the hormone levels to settle down. Cats who were spayed or neutered as adults sometimes need behavior modification to help correct spraying, because it has become habitual.

Take the cat to the vet to rule out any medical problems.

Behavior and Management Triggers

Poor litter-box management and inadequate clean-up of urine-targeted areas are two biggies that cause litter-box aversion. Another common trigger is the presence of neighborhood cats. Relationship issues between cats, including intercat aggression and the introduction of new cats, can cause cats to mark and to not use their boxes. Too many cats in too small of an area can tip the scales as well. Tension, stress, and changes in a household can cause cats to feel threatened. Sometimes, bringing in a new sofa or rearranging the furniture will cause cats to spray or miss their litter boxes. These are just some of the factors that can cause litter box issues. Because a thorough discussion of inappropriate elimination is outside the scope of this book, consider consulting with knowledgeable experts such as a certified cat-behavior consultant or a veterinary behaviorist if the situation seems unsolvable.

Good Litter-Box Management

Bad litter-box management is one of the most common reasons that cats develop litter-box issues. It is also one that can be easily addressed. The solution may lie in changing your litter-box locations and choices or changing your own habits.

Poor litter-box management is one of the most common reasons that cats sometimes won't use their boxes.

We think we have our cats' best interests in mind when carefully planning and setting up their restrooms. Many people think that cats want privacy, so they put the litter boxes in the closet or in the shower, or they provide the cats with covered boxes. Some cat people spend a fortune on cabinets or elaborate walk-in solutions where the boxes are hidden to all but the initiated. These

SYNTHETIC PHEROMONE DIFFUSERS

There are plug-in diffusers available that disperse a synthetic pheromone into the air; this can help take the edge off a cat's stress. The pheromones mimic natural cat pheromones that are perceived as friendly by other cats. The diffuser is not a magic solution and is most effective when used along with management and behavior modification. The information that is included with the diffuser will give full instructions and details on how to properly use the device.

hide-a-box solutions are also used to hide litter boxes and their smells from the human inhabitants and their guests.

Scented litters are also erroneously used because some people think that the scent will mask the odor of used cat litter. The scent may seem to a human to mask the odor, but a cat isn't fooled. Cat noses are highly tuned, and the smell of scented and dirty litter can cause litter-box aversion. Often, the people who resort to using scented litters don't clean the litter box every day or don't provide enough litter boxes for their cats, without understanding the consequences. Any of these situations can result in cats eliminating outside the litter box. The good news is that the problem is easily solvable with good litter-box management.

Litter-Box Solutions

Cats feel vulnerable when they eliminate because eliminating can be a potentially compromising situation for them. It would be easy for a predator or another cat to corner and ambush a cat while the cat is in the act of using the bathroom. Additionally, the accompanying odors can scare away potential food sources and attract that darned predator. Cats hate being in a situation where there is a possibility of being trapped. Do you blame them?

Covered boxes, hide-a-box solutions, and boxes in closets, under desks, and in showers create potential trap situations because they don't allow multiple escape routes. Instead of using those nice, clean, out-of-the-way boxes, many cats will eliminate in areas that feel safer for them, such as in the corner of the living room or on the couch. Another problem with covered boxes is that they keep the odors in. You might be a conscientious scooper, scooping after each use, but the smells still remain in the covered box or cabinet. Don't forget that cats have very sensitive noses and are capable of smelling much more than we humans can detect.

Electronic litter boxes are all the rage with some people but not popular with many cats. These boxes have their own set of problems. Most are too small for cats, and they make startling noises when they do their job. Additionally, some models have rakes and cleaning mechanisms that are hard

Make sure the litter box is large and deep enough for your cat.

to keep clean. If you are using automatic boxes and your cat prefers to eliminate elsewhere, consider resorting to an old-fashioned cat box and scooper.

In some cases, simply taking the cover off of the box isn't enough. The majority of commercial cat boxes are too small for our adult cats. Additionally, most are too shallow, sometimes resulting in more litter ending up outside of the box than inside. That being said, there are a couple of uncovered commercial litter boxes that are big, are deep, and have a snap-on piece around the edge of the box that adds a little height and helps keep the litter in the cat box. Another alternative solution that is perfect for most adult cats is the use of a translucent 66-quart storage container without its cover. The 12-inch height of the box keeps litter inside it, and cats can easily jump in and out without a problem. They can also see who is around and easily escape as needed.

The number of litter boxes and their locations are both very important. Remember, cats don't like to feel trapped, so instead of placing boxes in out-of-the-way locations, consider placing them where the cat can see the whole room, outside the door, and maybe down the hall. That way, the cat can feel safer when doing her business. Cats also need choices. The ideal situation is to provide one more box than there are cats. If you have three cats, ideally you should have four litter boxes located in different areas in the house. If you live in a small house, it might not be necessary to have that many boxes, but if your house has multiple levels, locate one box on each floor of the house. Later in this chapter, I discuss more litter-box solutions for multiple-cat households.

Kittens and special-needs cats need boxes that will work for their particular circumstances. Kittens need smaller, shallower boxes than adults, and more of them. There are also cats who have problems jumping; they may be arthritic, have age-related challenges, or have other physical limitations. These cats can do well with either the large under-bed storage boxes or with the previously mentioned 66-quart storage containers with one side cut down for accessibility.

Uncovered litter boxes can help stop litter-box problems. They allow cats to see potential threats and give the cats a choice of escape routes.

Cats can develop litter-box aversions because of painful or traumatic associations they have with the litter box. For example, they may have had a medical problem, such as a urinary-tract infection, that made urinating painful. Traumatic experiences such as being startled by a noise or ambushed by another cat while using the litter box can result in box aversion. After the trauma or medical problem has been resolved, the solution for these situations can consist of providing the cat with a whole new litter-box and kitty-litter experience. Provide your pain- or trauma-challenged cat with a different type of litter box and fill it with litter that is different from what she is used to using. Place the new box in the room with the original box, locating the new box strategically so that your cat won't feel trapped when using it. Don't remove the original box until the problem is resolved and the cat is consistently using the new box.

Large, translucent, 66-quart storage boxes are perfect litter-box solutions for most adult cats.

Cats, like most animals, don't like to eat where their bathrooms are located. You probably don't want to eat dinner in the bathroom. Neither do cats. Instinctually, cats eliminate away from their feeding areas, helping to keep predators from finding them. Check your litter-box locations and move the boxes away from feeding stations.

Scooping Rules

It's simple: scoop at least once a day. Additionally, dump the litter and wash out the box every few weeks. Three inches of new litter is sufficient. Whenever you add new boxes, put a cup or so of litter from the old boxes in the new boxes. Leave the existing boxes in their original locations, because cats need consistency. Once the cat is consistently using the new boxes, the original boxes can gradually be removed, one at a time.

Cat litter should be unscented. Many cats hate the smell of scented litter, and because the whole reason for this exercise is for cats to use their litter boxes, you need to make them happy. Buy unscented. If you use a clay-based litter,

Litter boxes need to be scooped at least once a day.

consider using Cat Attract, a scoopable clay litter. It has an additive in it that encourages cats to use their litter box.

Squeaky Clean

Cats will continue to eliminate in the same off-limits areas if the areas haven't been thoroughly cleaned. Soap and water alone isn't the answer. An area may smell fine to us, but remember that a cat's nose is more finely tuned than a human's nose. Identifying areas that have been targeted can

Boxes need to be emptied of litter, cleaned, and refilled with about 3 inches of fresh litter every three to four weeks.

sometimes be a challenge. A good black light, available in pet stores and online, can help. Turn all of the lights out and turn on the black light. Urine will fluoresce under a black light, showing you where you need to clean. To thoroughly clean an area so that even the sensitive nose of a cat can't detect the urine, an excellent enzyme cleaner is mandatory. Not all enzyme cleaners are created equal, though. Do your research to find the best one. Keep in mind also that even the best enzyme cleaner can't adequately clean porous areas that have been repeatedly saturated with urine. These are the extreme cases in which the only solution is a new mattress, sofa, or carpet.

SOMETIMES IT'S OBVIOUS

One of my cases concerned Sable, a beautiful, large, neutered male cat who was kept indoors. He was spraying the homeowner's living-room picture windows. Sable had done some major damage, destroying the rug as well as damaging the floor boards.

I arrived on the scene, armed with my enzyme cleaner. As I walked up the long driveway, I noticed lots of bowls filled with cat food in the lovely garden in front of the house. There were many happy cats gratefully taking advantage of the repast. Next, I saw the homeowner elegantly sipping her tea in the living room, enjoying herself, watching through the big picture windows as the feral cats enjoyed their feast. As I observed this peaceable kingdom, Sable sauntered up to the window, looked out, turned so his tail faced the window, and sprayed. It didn't take any sleuthing to uncover the reason he was spraying.

The Outsiders

Neighborhood cats can cause indoor cats to spray or not use their boxes.

Cats who happen to be strolling around your backyard can cause your cat to spray and urinate outside the cat box. It doesn't matter if the visitors are well cared for by the neighbors or if they are feral; their presence can upset your cat. Besides the vocalizing sometimes heard at the windows, it is usually easy to determine if outside visitors are causing your cat to have bathroom issues by the locations in which your cat is eliminating or spraying. Typically, cats who are responding to outsiders will target doors, windows, and the perimeters of the rooms nearest to the intruders.

To solve this problem, the outside cats need to be convinced not to hang out in your yard. There are many kinds of deterrents commercially available that can help. Choose carefully, as some of these products can compromise an animal's health while others are perfectly safe. One safe deterrent emits a sound that is undetectable to human ears, but heard by animals. Others are products that you spray on fences or sprinkle on soil. Lemon also works to an extent. There are many solutions available; just make sure that they will not hurt or poison the cats in any way. If you are purposely feeding the ferals at your house, finding a place to set up the feeding stations that is not viewable from your house may help.

If the outdoor cats belong to your neighbors, try to talk to them. Ask them politely to keep their cats inside. You may be able to sway them by explaining how vet bills are greatly reduced when cats are kept inside 24/7. You can also dazzle them with statistics about how indoor cats live much longer than cats who are allowed outside. If that doesn't work, try baking cookies. Good luck with that.

Feral cats can be trapped, neutered, and returned, though they will need to be managed so that they don't hang out near the house. If you are feeding them, set up feeding stations away from the house. Contact local feral-cat networks or your local animal shelter for guidance.

If you are feeding feral cats, move their feeding stations away from the house so that your resident cats can't see them.

Along with making your yard an undesirable place for unwelcome cats, you'll need to manage your environment and work with your indoor cats. Start by making it impossible for your cats to see outside. You can block the bottom portions of windows using thick paper or fabric. Be creative. If you have children, you can entertain them by having them draw and paint on the paper. The windows won't be blocked forever. The paper can be removed and your view restored after the problem has been resolved and the outside visitors have moved on. Who knows, maybe your spraying cats will be the inspiration for the next Leonardo da Vinci or Jackson Pollock.

Cleanup is vital. Not only do you need to make sure that the inside of the house is free of urine but you will also have to thoroughly clean the outsides of doors, walls, and windows that could be targeted. It is common for outside visitors to leave calling cards, spraying on the exterior of your house. Your cat's highly tuned nose can pick up the scent of urine from inside the house. Spend a moonless night outside, armed with a black light and a really good enzyme cleaner. Pay attention to the corners, sides, and bottoms of sliding glass doors and windows. These can be favorite places for cats to spray.

The Multiple-Cat Factor

Some cats have relationship challenges resulting in inappropriate elimination. The cats may have been introduced to each other too fast, or there might be too many cats in too small of a space with little or no vertical territory. Or maybe the cats simply don't like each other. Cats sometimes leave calling cards when they don't feel confident around other cats, or they may be leaving information about themselves for other cats to discover. Poor litter-box management can be a big contributing factor in this situation, as well.

Cats sometimes avoid their litter boxes because of relationship challenges with other cats in the household.

Make sure that there are enough clean boxes in different locations around the house. You want to provide a situation in which the cats feel safe when using the litter boxes. Cats are very good at staking out areas as theirs. If the litter boxes are located in one cat's particular domain, another cat might be afraid to trespass in order to use the box.

To solve the litter-box problem in a multiple-cat situation, the causes behind the behavior have to be addressed. If your cats are having difficulties with a new cat who has come to stay, reintroduce the cats to each other slowly, following the steps outlined in chapter 5. Chapter 6 focuses on a few types of aggression, including intercat aggression, which is a biggie for litter-box aversion.

After Cleanup

No matter what is causing the cats to spray or not use their boxes, a thorough cleanup with an excellent enzyme cleaner is mandatory. After cleaning up, change the cat's experience with the targeted inappropriate area by engaging her in activities she enjoys there so that she doesn't see it as a bathroom or place to spray. If your cat enjoys playing, then play with her on the once-soiled area. Clicker training, feeding her snacks, and grooming her in the locations she had previously targeted will help change how she views those areas. Whatever the activities are, she needs to enjoy them. If she is having issues with other cats, make sure that the other cats are in another room while you have your quality one-on-one time with her.

Scratching posts placed strategically can help change your cat's perspective of the target area.

Scratching posts and horizontal scratchers can also be placed in the once-soiled areas to change the cat's view of the target areas. Because cats mark by scratching, placing the poles and horizontal scratchers on the areas will provide the cat with a more acceptable way of delineating her territory and broadcasting information about herself to other cats.

Clicker Training with Inappropriate Elimination

Clicker training in combination with the other suggestions can help stop inappropriate elimination. It is important to note though that the clicker approach used for litter-box issues is different than the clicker techniques used to solve other unwanted behaviors in this book. When working with other behaviors, clicker training is used to reward and communicate when the cat is engaged in an approved behavior. That approach isn't recommended for litter-box issues because clicking a cat while she is in the act of using the litter box can interrupt the business at hand, changing her focus to the click and treat. It can be done, but it's tricky and subtle. The timing is crucial, and depending on the cat and the situation, there can be varying results, including the cat not using the litter box unless her favorite person is there and the cat jumping out of the box to receive her treats. Needless to say, these are not our goal behaviors.

Clicker training helps cats feel secure and strengthens bonds between cats and their people.

Clicker Therapy for Cats

Using clicker training to help solve inappropriate elimination works similar to therapy. It builds confidence in cats, helping them feel safe and secure and relieve tensions. It also builds and strengthens bonds between cats and their people, helping to increase feelings of security and consistency. Confident, happy cats are more apt to use their litter boxes.

Clicker-training therapy redirects cats away from the situation that was causing them not to use their box by providing them with fun alternative behaviors. Cats who have out-of-the-box issues due to intercat relationship challenges benefit from clicker training, which both refocuses the warring cats and helps create positive experiences between them. The details on how to click away aggression can be found in chapter 6.

Clicker training is great for helping to relieve stress and tension. This is crucial in litter-box aversion because many litter-box issues develop from cats being stressed. Clicker-training therapy helps because it builds confidence and security, focuses the cat away from the cause of the behavior, and, when practiced on a daily basis, gives the cat the consistency she needs.

Clicker training is helpful for changing a cat's association with the areas that have been eliminated or sprayed on. After cleaning the area thoroughly with a good enzyme cleaner, the guilty cat can be taught tricks in the targeted locations. The object of the exercise is for the cat to now see the area she previously eliminated on as a place to play, learn, or eat.

Clicker training can help a cat feel secure and confident. Often, inappropriate elimination challenges occur because of inconsistencies in the household. A few examples include new furniture, remodeling, a change in schedules, a new family member, or a move. When a

Clicker training helps relieve the stress that can cause litter-box aversion.

cat's world is shaken by changes, she sometimes develops litter-box issues. Cats with intercat issues and shy cats can also benefit from clicker training; it increases their confidence and feelings of security so that they won't have reasons to mark or avoid their litter boxes. Additionally, daily and consistent sessions will give cats something to look forward to and increase the bonds they have with their people.

CLICKER THERAPY FOR CATS

Clicker training:
- Builds confidence and security.
- Refocuses cats away from the causes of the behavior.
- Changes the association with the targeted areas.
- Provides cats with alternative behaviors.
- Builds and strengthens relationships.

Magic Clicks

There aren't any magic clicker tricks that will stop inappropriate elimination. It's the clicker-training process—the consistent sessions and the fun factor of clicker training—along with management and environmental changes, that will help stop the behavior. Every cat is an individual. Depending on each cat's situation and the causes of her behavior, it usually doesn't matter what tricks you teach the cat as long as the interaction is fun for everyone.

Dealing with Frustration

Cats going to the bathroom on the sofa, on the clean laundry, or in the corner can be very frustrating situations. If you find that you're at the end of your rope, consider reaching out for help and consulting with people who specialize in feline behavioral problems. A certified cat-behavior consultant or a veterinary behaviorist can help you identify the reasons your cat is not using the litter box or is spraying and can help you resolve the problem.

Inappropriate elimination is a behavior challenge that frustrates everyone in the household.

Case Study: Inappropriate Elimination

SITUATION: Annapurna, a large, two-year-old longhaired female, was urinating and sometimes defecating outside the litter box. Her favorite places to urinate were in and in back of two bathtubs. She and her companion, a three-year-old fluffy female named Talia, shared two small covered boxes. One of the boxes was located in a closet in an upstairs bathroom, the other in a shower stall in a downstairs bathroom. Both cats were well cared for, loved, and showered with affection by the whole family. The cats were taken to the groomer on a regular basis and were combed and fluffed every day by the two young daughters. Both cats had been declawed.

The home where the family lived was a large three-story house. Earlier in the year, the family had to temporarily relocate while the house was remodeled and expanded. Shortly after moving back into the newly remodeled house, Annapurna started to urinate in the bathtub.

ASSESSMENT: The stress of the remodeling along with poor litter-box locations, not enough litter boxes, and boxes that were too small caused the improper elimination. Annapurna was feeling insecure because of the inconsistencies in her environment due to the remodeling of the house. This insecurity was compounded by the fact that the litter-box locations didn't provide escape routes and the boxes were too small for such large cats.

RECOMMENDATIONS:

I recommended a combination of improved litter-box management, a thorough cleanup with an excellent enzyme cleaner, consistent schedules for feeding and playtime, and clicker training. Three new large, uncovered, translucent storage containers were placed in areas that had good escape potential. One box was located in an alcove that afforded a view of the living room and the kitchen. Another box was placed upstairs where the cats could see the entrances of the bedrooms and the hall. A third box was placed in the bathroom where Annapurna was having the most litter-box challenges. The original boxes were temporarily kept in place.

The whole family got involved with Annapurna's rehabilitation. The two children played with both cats using a fishing-pole toy. The play extended into the targeted areas in the bathroom. They also clicker-trained Annapurna, teaching her to sit and shake hands on cue.

The family also kept Annapurna on a regular schedule. They fed her at the same time every day, groomed her every evening, and played with and clicker-trained her on a schedule. The schedule, as well as the attention, helped Annapurna feel a little more secure and relaxed with the recent household changes. It did take time and consistency, but Annapurna gradually stopped using the bathtubs as litter boxes and went back to consistently using the provided boxes.

Tricks

It's impressive to watch cats shake hands, jump over poles, and perform other tricks. Besides the satisfaction of proving to the rest of the world that cats can easily be trained, teaching cats tricks helps increase their confidence, redirects them from problem behaviors, challenges them, and builds and strengthens relationships between them and the people they live with.

There's a wide range of tricks that cats can learn. Be creative and have fun, but teach tricks that are extensions of natural behaviors. For instance, cats jump and climb, so teaching them to jump over poles and climb ladders is a natural extension. They also flop, so you can ask them to play dead or lie down with visual (such as hand signals) and/or verbal cues.

THE TRICK TOOL KIT

- Primary reinforcer (treats)
- Secondary reinforcer (clicker)
- Target (pencil or chopstick)
- Stool
- Pole and hoops
- Toys

Don't ask them to do tricks that are not based in natural behaviors. For instance, cats don't normally walk tightropes or wires; they also don't balance things on their sensitive noses. These behaviors can be difficult and stressful for cats. When teaching your cats tricks, don't forget rule number one: it needs to be fun for everyone—especially your cat.

Also, think ahead and consider the possible consequences of the tricks you ask your cat to perform. You can teach your cat how to turn the lights on and off, how to open drawers, or how to flush the toilet. Think it through, though. Many cats can get a little too enthusiastic with their newfound talents. Do you want your cat to start turning the lights on when you're away for the day or in the middle of the night? Or to flush the toilet repeatedly and cause your water bill to skyrocket? The tricks need to be behaviors that you're comfortable with the cat performing at unexpected times.

It goes without saying that before you can teach your cat tricks, she will need to know the basics of clicker training. Because many tricks build on others, your cat will need to know other clicker-trained behaviors, as well, such as sitting on a stool and waiting on cue.

Shaking Hands

Shaking hands is an entertaining and impressive trick. Not too many people can boast of walking up to a cat, extending a hand, and having it met with a paw. It's a fun trick to teach, though it may take a few sessions until your cat can successfully perform it. Before learning to shake hands, your cat needs to be able to sit on cue. Details on how to teach her to sit are covered in chapter 2.

Teaching your cat to shake hands can be accomplished through a few clicker techniques. After cuing her into a *sit*, watch her. If your cat happens to raise her right

FETCH!

Sudan, my Savannah, loves to fetch. He will fetch for hours. I did not teach him to fetch; he's a natural fetcher. One day, he brought me his favorite cloth banana. Because I think cats who fetch are cool, I captured the behavior with a click and a treat and continued to reinforce it each time he brought me his banana. Because Sudan loves the attention and he loves to fetch, the game itself became the reward.

Sudan takes every opportunity to play a rollicking game of fetch with me. It doesn't matter if I'm sitting at the computer writing this book or eating breakfast, Sudan will seek me out and drop his banana somewhere I'm sure to notice. This morning, he dropped it in my cup of tea.

paw up, capture the movement with a click and then immediately give her a treat. In clicker-speak, this is called *capturing behavior.* It's a way of reinforcing a naturally occurring behavior without a prompt or cue.

Each time she raises her paw, click and treat her. Add the visual cue of extending your right open palm to her left paw. Depending on how eager the cat is to learn, this technique can take many repetitions until she understands that raising her paw is reinforced and rewarded with a click and a treat.

Before you can teach your cat how to shake hands, she will need to know how to sit on request for a short length of time.

Shaping is another effective clicker-training technique. Shaping behaviors is subtler and involves clicking and then treating for minute movements that move closer and closer to the goal behavior. At first, the movement might only be a simple shift of weight in preparation for lifting the paw, or a slight elevation of the paw. Just as she is raising her paw or shifting her weight while still sitting, mark the event with a click and then treat her. Every time a movement takes her successively closer to shaking hands, click and treat. It can take many repetitions and a couple of sessions until she starts lifting her paw up to the level you want.

Be patient, and shape in baby steps. Don't forget the visual cue of extending your palm toward her paw. Because shaking hands is done right-handed and right-pawed, make sure that you click and treat only when her right paw is moving. If she moves her left paw, or doesn't move at all, don't click and don't treat.

You can also first prompt her to raise her paw by touching her right paw with your right hand. If she's a typical cat, she'll respond by lifting her paw. The slightest paw movement upward needs to be shaped with a click as it's occurring. Your extended hand will become the cue for shaking hands.

Whatever method you use to train her to shake hands, the visual cue should be extending an open palm that faces left, toward your cat's right paw. When she raises her paw to meet your hand, click and treat. After she correctly shakes hands eight out of ten times, add a verbal cue such as *shake hands* or *hello* as you extend your hand toward her paw.

Be careful that you don't become sloppy and create a training problem by accidentally clicking when your cat puts her paw up while moving around or standing up. It's easy to get excited while training cats. You might click a perfect paw move but forget that the cat is supposed to be sitting down while she is raising her paw to your hand.

Click and treat for each small movement that takes your cat closer to the goal behavior of shaking hands.

Cats are individuals; they learn at their own pace. If your cat seems stuck and just not picking up on what you're asking, review your methods. You may need to take smaller steps while shaping the behavior for her to learn the new behavior. Or, perhaps you are clicking too slowly or too soon. Maybe the treat isn't motivating enough, or maybe your clicks are too random for your little Einstein and you aren't shaping toward the final behavior goal.

CAN YOU TEACH AN OLD CAT NEW TRICKS?

Maulee is a fifteen-year-old clicker-trained Bengal who I started clicker-training when she was twelve. Maulee loves clicker training. Every afternoon before dinner, she sits on her favorite stool, waiting for her daily lesson. Some of Maulee's favorite tricks and behaviors are sitting, staying, and finding my keys on cue. Clicker training is keeping her young and active. She's very clever, catching on to new behaviors immediately. So yes, you can teach an old cat new tricks.

High Five

Teaching your cat to do high fives after she learns to shake hands is easy. Instead of holding your hand low for the handshake, raise your hand higher, clicking and treating when her paw makes contact with your hand. Using the baby-step shaping technique, gradually

After your cat shakes hands eight out of ten times, add a verbal cue. Say "shake" as you give her your hand to shake.

raise your hand up to the high-five position, clicking and treating her each time her paw meets your hand. If your cat doesn't connect with your hand, don't click.

Now that your cat has learned how to shake hands, it's easy to teach her to high five on request.

Instead, go back to a comfortable level and proceed more slowly. You may find that you need to shorten the length of the training sessions and increase the number of shorter sessions you do throughout the day.

When your cat does connect with your hand eight out of ten times in a row, add a verbal cue such as *high five* or *give me five*. Be creative in your cues. Whatever word you use, don't change it. Consistency is important. Being creative and using an unusual verbal cue adds a little spice to the behavior and makes it more entertaining for your audience.

Pole Jumping

Requesting that your cat sit before jumping over a pole looks polished and professional.

Before teaching your cat to jump over a pole, you'll need the right prop. In this case, the prop is a simple pole. You can be innovative when finding the perfect pole for your cat. A wooden dowel of 1 to 2 inches in diameter will work. Hollow cardboard tubes used for wrapping paper are also great for this trick. The first object I converted into a jumping pole was a cardboard tube that I wrapped with leopard-spotted paper for effect. It was perfect.

Because you want to wow your audience, have a beginning to each trick. Starting the pole-jumping trick with your cat in a sitting position looks polished and formal. Start simple. First, ask your cat to sit, then place the pole on the floor for your cat to walk over. As she walks over it, capture the behavior by clicking and immediately treating. If your cat doesn't walk over the pole, tap the target on the other side of the pole. By now your cat is well target-trained and will walk over the pole toward the target. Just as she completes her walk over the pole, click her and then treat her, tossing the treat on the correct side of the pole.

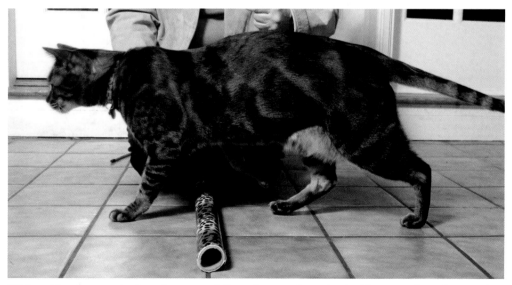

Click and treat your cat when she successfully walks over the pole. At this stage, the pole is on the floor.

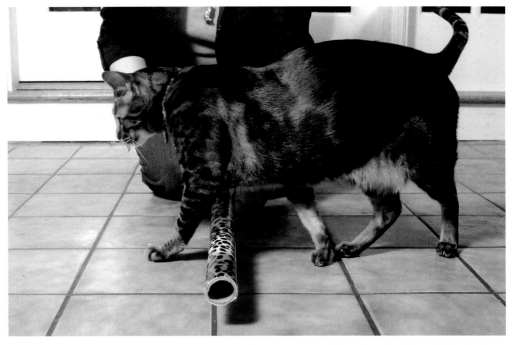

Gradually increase the pole's distance from the floor. Start by raising the pole about half an inch off the floor.

Don't let her touch the target, because the target is not the cue. The target is only for jump-starting her on the way to pole-jumping stardom and needs to be phased out after a couple of repetitions. As your Hollywood cat is eating her treat, pick up the pole so that you can reset the behavior, cuing her to walk over the pole again by placing it back on the floor after she's eaten her treat. You are ready for the next step after your cat successfully walks over the pole repeatedly whenever she is cued by your placing the pole in front of her. Don't forget to click and then treat each time she walks across the pole.

The next step in teaching the pole jump is to hold the pole about half an inch above the floor. The pole is the visual cue for her to perform. Click and treat when she completes her walk over the slightly elevated pole. While she is eating her treat, remove the pole from her vision so that you can reset the behavior cycle. If your cat doesn't step over the elevated pole, place the pole on the floor and start from the beginning, using the 300 Peck Pigeon method covered in chapter 3.

Continue to practice with her at the basic level of stepping over the pole, visually cuing her by positioning the pole in front of her. Gradually raise the pole higher by very small increments after your cat successfully steps or jumps over the lower heights, clicking and then treating her after she's completed the jump.

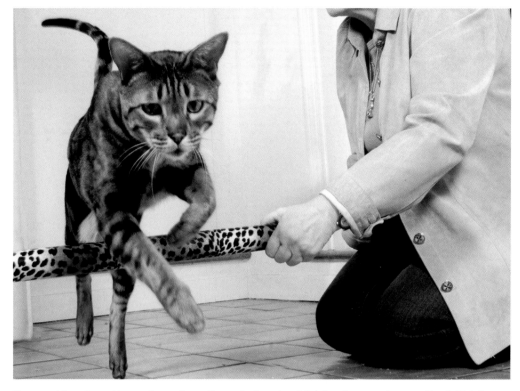

Every cat is unique. Your cat may learn the pole-jumping trick in a few sessions, or it might take a series of sessions over a few weeks.

Eventually, the pole will be at a height where your cat can go under instead of over it. Don't be discouraged if she does decide to take the low road. After all, it's easier to walk underneath an elevated pole than to jump over it. If that happens, don't click and treat her. Instead, lower the pole down to a level that she has consistently been jumping over and then slowly increase the distance from the floor until she finally jumps consistently over the pole at the desired height.

Add the verbal cue *jump* only after your cat jumps over the elevated pole eight out of ten times. As you are visually cuing her by holding the pole in position, say "jump." Make sure to click after she's jumped over the pole and then treat her.

Teaching your cat to jump over a pole will probably take several small sessions over a period of days or even weeks. It depends on your cat, your techniques, and your clicker-training schedule.

Keep your cat's limitations in mind. Some cats are master jumpers, enjoying the high jump; others may be older, or their idea of the high jump is leaping up to the sofa to snuggle with their favorite person. Ask your cat to leap poles only at heights that are reasonable for her.

Chain of Events

Now that your cat has a strong pole-jumping technique, you can become creative and combine behaviors and substitute props. Instead of jumping over a pole, consider presenting your cat with a hoop to jump through. After she is successful with leaping through hoops, you can gradually decrease the size of the hoops for her to jump through. Or you can pretend she's a circus lion and decorate the hoop with strips of shiny paper.

Jumping through a hoop can be chained with other behaviors, such as sitting at the beginning and end of the trick.

In addition to substituting props, behaviors can be combined. In clicker-speak, this is called *chaining*. Your cat can be trained to first sit, then jump through a hoop placed between two stools, and then sit again to complete the behavior sequence. Start by placing two stools about 18 inches apart. Cue your cat to sit on the first stool; mark the event with a click, treating her as she sits on the stool. It looks finished and professional to both start and end this multiple-part trick with a *sit*. After the cat is sitting, use the verbal cue *jump*. Just as your cat lands on the second stool, click her and then treat her on the stool. You may also have to visually cue her to jump by tapping the target on the stool. Cue her to sit again, click, and treat. Start over. At this stage of learning, the hoop is not placed between the stools.

Don't forget to click and treat your cat as she performs the last *sit* in the behavior chain. This click applies to the whole chain.

After she successfully sits, jumps, and finishes the sequence with a *sit* eight out of ten times, change when you click and treat. Start by cuing her into a sit. Do not click and treat her. After she sits, immediately give her the cue to jump. Again, don't click and treat her, even though she does as requested. Instead, after she lands on the stool, cue her to

Once your cat is easily jumping through the hoop, gradually increase the distance between the stools.

sit, and then click her just as she does her final *sit*; follow the click with a treat. Because the click indicates the end of the behavior, click her only after she completes the whole sequence of sitting, jumping, and sitting again.

It may take a few sessions until she successfully executes the three behaviors. If she is having problems completing the whole sequence, then chain only the first two behaviors together, clicking and treating after the jump. Then cue her for the last sit, clicking and treating when she performs it correctly. After she is proficient in the separate behaviors, begin to click and treat her only after all three behaviors are successfully completed as a chain. Now you can live dangerously and add the hoops.

Hold the hoop between the stools so that, in order to jump to the other stool, she has to jump through the hoop. After she is comfortable with the behavior and does it correctly eight out of ten times consecutively, you can gradually extend the distance between the stools. Don't put too much space between the stools; the trick needs to be safe for your cat. Eventually, the whole trick sequence can become a little act, complete with drum rolls, music, and a performance program.

Make sure to click after the last behavior and then give your cat an extra-delicious treat for successfully completing the whole sequence.

Here's an outline of the behaviors you're chaining together:

1. Sitting
2. Jumping to the other stool, through the hoop
3. Sitting on the second stool after jumping through the hoop

Fetching

It can be challenging to train your cat to fetch. Some cats are natural fetchers and will instigate fetching games without our help. Other cats need to be worked with, the behavior shaped and captured through clicker training. The most effective time to have a fetching session is before mealtimes, when your cat is more motivated to work. If your cat doesn't catch on right away, that's OK. Remember rule number one: clicker training should be fun for you and your cat.

The best time to train your cat to fetch is right before mealtimes, when she will eagerly work for her favorite treats.

The Reluctant Fetcher

If you have a cat who doesn't occasionally carry a favorite toy around in her mouth, she is probably a reluctant fetcher. You can train her to fetch through baby steps. First, find an appropriate toy that she will eagerly carry. Identify toy favoritism by tossing toys toward her and gauging her responses. If she prefers one toy over another, then always use that toy for the fetching lessons. If your cat doesn't have much interest in toys, give her a soft toy that she can comfortably hold in her mouth but not swallow. You can cheat a little by rubbing some tuna juice or another flavorful broth that your cat adores on the toy.

THE BEST TOY FOR THE JOB

A good fetching object is something that's easy and comfortable for your cat to pick up in her mouth. It has to be safe and unbreakable, one that she can't swallow or chew pieces off of. Some soft balls and toys work well for the job. Cats sometimes pick their own favorite toys to fetch. Sudan, my Savannah, prefers to fetch a cloth banana. Olivia, a little Bengal, has a couple of mice she likes to play fetch with. Maulee loves a spotted knot that looks a little like her. Every cat is different and has individual preferences. Your cat may choose the toy for you to throw by bringing it to you.

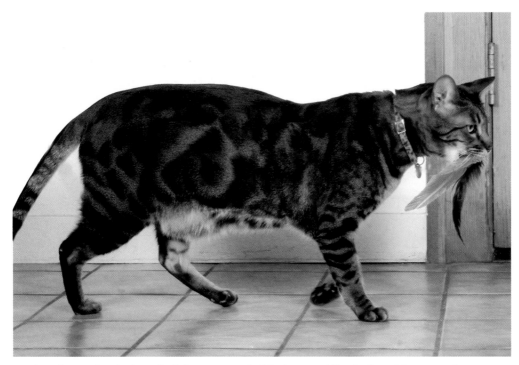

Work on increasing the length of time your cat holds the toy while she is walking toward you.

Jump-start the fetching trick by tossing the toy a short distance past your cat, at her eye level. Her natural inclination will be to follow it with her eyes and chase it. If you've cheated and put a flavorful broth on it, she will be more motivated to chase it and put it in her mouth.

Some cats will pick up the toy and walk toward you, others will only smell it, and still others will put their mouths on the toy. Whatever your cat does with the toy is where you begin. If she happens to only smell it, then click and reward her. If she picks it up in her mouth, then click and reward that. She may be one of these cats who's already halfway to becoming a fetching queen, picking it up and walking back toward you with the toy still in her mouth. If so, click and treat the fetching queen.

After you click and reward her for her interaction with the toy, pick up the toy. Wait for her to finish the treat, then toss the toy the same way you did previously. If she only touches it with her mouth, click and treat her. You want to click her for every small step toward picking it up. If you find that she eagerly picks up the toy, work on the duration of time for which she holds the toy in her mouth while walking toward you. After your cat picks up the toy, wait maybe half of a second or a full second while she is holding the toy in her mouth before clicking and rewarding her. If she moves toward you while she is holding the toy, click and treat.

Maybe you can cheat a little by getting the target out and asking her to follow it toward you. Keep in mind that the use of the target needs to be stopped as soon as your cat understands the behavior. We don't want your cat thinking that the target is her cue for bringing the toy to you. If she drops the toy but is walking toward you, do not click and treat. Only click and treat if she is carrying the toy while moving toward you.

Gradually increase the distance that your cat has to go to pick the toy up and bring it back to you.

Be patient; it is normal for some cats not to catch on right away. Just restart the training at a level where she performed correctly and comfortably. It can take many sessions until the reluctant fetcher gets the hang of it. Consider shortening the sessions and having more of them. Additionally, your cat may have gotten so many treats that she's no longer motivated to work, preferring to take a nice nap by the window. That's fine—she deserves a recess; she's been working hard. You can continue your sessions later in the day or the next day.

After your cat comes to you with the object in her mouth, touch the object with your hand and immediately click and reward her. She will drop the toy to eat the treat. After she releases the toy, pick it up. When she's finished eating the treat, throw the toy again, this time a little further away from her. Gradually build up the distance that she has to go to get the toy and bring it back to you. As usual, add a verbal cue only after she understands the behavior. As you throw the toy for her, say "fetch." With practice, your cat can become a fetching queen.

Just the Beginning

There are many complex and fun tricks that you can teach your cat. Use your imagination and combine them with interesting verbal cues and props. Never forget rule number one, though. It should always be fun for everyone; you, your audience, and especially the cat.

Clicker Training Over Time

The history and science that clicker training and the positive-training revolution are based on are impressive. The art and science of clicker training are not static and they continue to evolve beyond what is illustrated in this time line.

1930s: B.F. Skinner discovers the principles of operant conditioning and operant behavior.

1935: Skinner understands practical applications of operant conditioning for training animals.

1938-1943: Marian and Keller Breland are Skinner's first graduate students and research assistants.

1942-1943: The Brelands assist B.F. Skinner training pigeons to guide bombs during World War II.

1943: The Brelands start Animal Behavior Enterprises (ABE), an animal training business based on B.F. Skinner's operant conditioning principles.

1943-1944: The Brelands first use party clickers as secondary reinforcers.

1947: Marian Breland writes the first operant conditioning manual.

1950s: The Brelands create the first dog-training kit, which include a combination clicker and food delivery system.

1955: The Brelands open IQ Zoo in Arkansas, showcasing animals trained through operant conditioning.

1950s-1960s: Marine mammal and bird trainers start using operant conditioning training techniques.

1955: The Brelands write the first dolphin-training manual.

1962: U.S. Navy hires the Brelands to teach their trainers; students include Bob Bailey.

1963: Karen Pryor starts training dolphins at Sea Life Park in Hawaii using operant conditioning methods.

1964: Bob Bailey, the U.S. Navy's first director of training, trains the first dolphin for the Navy.

1965: Bob Bailey joins ABE as research director; he later becomes general manager.

1971: Karen Pryor resigns from Sea Life Park, consults for dolphin behavior projects, and starts writing.

1975: Karen Pryor, publishes *Lads before the Wind*.

1984: Karen Pryor publishes *Don't Shoot the Dog*.

1990: Marian and Bob Bailey retire ABE but continue to consult and teach.

1992: Karen Pryor, Gary Wilkes and Ingrid Shallenberger conduct the first clicker training seminar in San Francisco.

1992: The clicker training/operant conditioning method of training starts to gain acceptance.

1992 to present day: Karen Pryor educates through books, articles, conferences, videos and her popular web site: www.clickertraining.com

Present day: Bob Bailey continues to teach clicker training to students in Europe and Japan.

Resources

Recommended Reading

Bailey, Robert and Arthur Gillaspy, "Operant Psychology Goes to the Fair: Marian and Keller Breland in the Popular Press, 1947–1966," *The Behavior Analyst* 28 (2005):143–159.

Bailey, Robert and Marian Bailey. *Patient Like a Chipmunk*. DVD. Eclectic Science Productions, 1994.

Johnson-Bennett, Pam. *Starting from Scratch*. New York: Penguin Books. 2007

Kurland, Alexandra. *Clicker Training for Your Horse*. Waltham, MA: Sunshine Books, 2007.

Pryor, Karen. *Lads before the Wind*. Waltham, MA: Sunshine Books, 2000.

_____. *Don't Shoot the Dog*. New York: Bantam Books, 1999.

_____. *Reaching the Animal Mind*. New York: Scribner, 2009.

Skinner, B.F. *The Behavior Organisms: An Experimental Analysis*. Acton, MA: Copley Publishing Group, 2006.

Web Sites of Interest

The following Web sites and products are recommended by the author and do not reflect any endorsement by BowTie, Inc. Products are available in most pet supply stores unless otherwise indicated. See individual Web Sites for purchasing information and/or participating providers.

www.angelicalcat.com
Angelical Cat manufactures cat trees, condos, and houses.

www.animalbehavior.org
Official Web site of the Animal Behavior Society, which includes information on feline aggression.

www.avidid.com
Web site provides information on micro-chipping and the Avid brand of microchip.

www.behavior1.com
Bob Bailey's Web site, which provides information about cat agility.

www.behaviorworks.org
Behavior analyst Dr. Susan Friedman's official Web site.

www.bfskinner.org
Official Web Site of the B.F. Skinner Foundation, which includes information on operant conditioning.

www.berganexperience.com

Bergan manufactures pet products, including the Turbo Scratcher, a ball-in-track toy with a corrugated cardboard center.

www.catagility.com

The iCat Agility Web site, which provides information about cat agility.

http://catdancer.com

Cat Dancer manufactures pet products, including the Original Cat Dancer interactive toy.

www.clickertraining.com

Karen Pryor's official Web Site, where you can purchase the i-Click clicker.

www.cosmicpet.com

Cosmic Pet manufactures pet products, including the Cosmic Catnip Alpine Scratcher.

www.dacvb.org

The official Web site of the American Veterinary Society of Animal Behaviorists, which includes information on feline aggression.

www.felinefurniture.com

Feline Furniture manufactures modular cat furniture.

http://furwoodforest.com

Furwood Forest manufactures custom cat trees.

www.iaabc.org

The official Web site of the International Association of Behavior Consultants, which includes information on certified members specializing in solving the behavioral problems of cats, dogs, horses, and parrots.

www.nina-ottosson.com

Information on this designer of puzzle toys and her products, including the Dog Brick, Dog Spinney, and Dog Tornado, all of which can be used with cats.

www.petmate.com

Pet Mate manufactures pet products, including the Double Door Delux Kennel Pet Carrier.

www.premier.com

Premier manufactures a line of pet products.

http://public.homeagain.com

The Web site provides information on microchipping and the HomeAgain brand of microchip.

www.purrfectpost.com

Purrfect Post manufactures scratching posts.

http://stickypaws.com

Sticky Paws manufactures pet products, including the double-sided tape used to dissuade cats from scratching furniture.

www.theclickercenter.com

Alexandra Kurland's official Web site, which provides books and information on the 300 Peck Pigeon training method.

Index

About the Author

Marilyn Krieger, nationally known Certified Cat-Behavior Consultant, helps resolve cat-behavior issues using positive and humane methods, modifying behavior through clicker training and altering the cat's environment. In addition to writing cat behavior columns for both *Cat Fancy* magazine and *Catchannel.com*, Marilyn has published articles and columns in *USA Today*, *Catnip* (Tufts University School of Veterinary Medicine publication), and *Cats USA* as well as other journals. She also frequently appears as a guest on television and radio programs, providing valuable tips and insight on how to improve cat behavior. More information about Marilyn is available on her Web site: www.thecatcoach.com.

Photo Credits

AresT/Shutterstock.com: 73

Courtesy of the B.F. Skinner Foundation: 16

Jennifer Calvert: 132

Cioli & Hunnicutt/BowTie Studio: 1–15, 47–49 (top), 50, 64, 65, 69–71, 74–80, 86, 87 (bottom), 96–101, 102 (bottom), 103, 105–107, 115, 116, 120, 122 (top), 124–129, 130 (bottom), 133, 134, 137

P.J. Hoffmann: 33

Cris Kelly/BowTie: 12, 17–32, 34–38, 41–46, 49 (bottom), 51–60, 66–68, 81–85, 87 (top), 88–95, 102 (top), 104, 110–114, 117, 118, 122 (bottom), 130 (top), 131, 140–153

Pavel Sazonov/Shutterstock.com: 139

Rhonda Van: 40, 63, 135, 136

Don Wright: 9